How I Sold
My Business

a personal diary

ALVIN ALEXANDER

How I Sold My Business: A Personal Diary

Copyright 2014 Alvin J. Alexander

First edition, published February, 2014

To Kim

Who gave me the time to learn my craft,
and never discouraged my crazy ideas,
including the idea of starting my own business.

To Many Others

Who helped our business succeed.

After receiving a letter in the mail one day in the fall of 2002, I made a decision to investigate the idea of selling my company, a small business I originally founded in 1994.

Once I decided to explore this, I did what I normally do when faced with any big decision: *A lot of research*. While I usually like to talk to as many people as I can about important business decisions, in this case I didn't think I could talk to anyone about what I was doing, so instead I bought several books related to the process of selling a business.

All the books I found were written by accountants and business valuators who shared different formulas related to valuing a business. By using all those formulas I learned the "secret" that my company was worth somewhere between $300K and $5M. Um, thanks guys, that really narrowed it down.

Besides not being helpful in valuing my business, it didn't seem like any of those books were written by business owners, and they didn't write about the *process* of selling a business, it was all just formulas. Besides the worth of my company, I had many questions, things like:

- How do you really go about selling your company? How do you put it "on the market?"
- What is a business broker? How do you find one and work with one?
- What are the pros and cons of putting my business up for sale?
- What if my competitors or employees find out my business is for sale?
- Do you have regrets after the sale? If so, what are they?

Once I made the decision to put my business on the market, I wrote down many small notes before and after meetings with business brokers, lawyers, potential buyers, and even my business partners. At some point in the process all those little notes turned into a diary, and after the sale, that diary turned into a small website. Based on the feedback and encouragement I received there, that website became this book -- the book I wish I could have read before I put my business up for sale.

Note: As the old saying goes, this story is based on actual events. However, in certain cases, incidents, characters and timelines have been changed for dramatic purposes. Certain characters may be composites, or entirely fictitious.

HOW I SOLD MY BUSINESS

BACKGROUND

Background

Before jumping into the diary, there is some background material that I need to cover to provide some context for the diary itself. I'll cover only the items I think are essential to knowing me, and my company.

I graduated from college with a B.S. Degree in Aerospace Engineering in 1984, but even then, I knew that I didn't want to be an "Engineer." Despite my ability to work through all the formulas better than most other students, I never had a physical feel for engineering. Fortunately things worked out for me, and although I was hired as an engineer, I was also given a lot of duties related to the company's new computers and network. In short order I was managing all the DOS-based personal computers for our company, including our network.

While that transition couldn't have worked out better for me, I still became disenchanted, feeling like just another cog in the machinery at a large company. Even though my yearly raises were always 10% or more, a $50K salary four years after graduating college just wasn't increasing fast enough for my financial ambitions.

After a few false starts, I began working for a regional computer consulting firm, where my salary went from $50K to more than $100K in less than three years. However, unhappy with several issues at that firm, I left that company, lived out a one-year "non competition agreement," and started my own computer consulting company in Louisville, Kentucky in 1994.

I read some books about the legal process of starting a company, interviewed a few local accountants and business attorneys I found in the Yellow Pages, and started my new business from the basement of my house. I got a dedicated phone line, had some business cards made, created some stationery, learned how to use QuickBooks and a little more about accounting than I already knew (I started off as a business major in college), called some old contacts, and I was in business.

With the internet taking off, along with my experience with DOS, Windows, Mac and Unix computer systems and my contacts in the local business world (which admittedly came from my previous employer), I lucked into the perfect time to start a computer consulting business. With the work flowing in, my wife came on board as Employee #2, taking over the bookkeeping duties, some office duties, and handling the flood of incoming sales calls that comes with opening a new business.

With just as much good luck, I was also able to hire some talented people right away, one who could help with the technical work, and another who could take over sales. A fellow techie named David joined me right away (followed by some other people who didn't last long), and I was also fortunate to hire a good salesperson named Jack who I had worked with before.

While my ego would like to take credit for the growth of the company, truthfully the only credit I can take is when I applied the old adage "hire well" to the company. Once I followed the advice of "Don't be afraid to hire people that are smarter/better than you are," I didn't have to babysit my employees all the time, and we began quite a roll.

Fast-forward from that time until just before the dot-com bust in 2000, and life was good. Our business had grown to fifteen full-time employees and a few part-time contractors, and sales had just crossed over $2M in the last two years. Our biggest problems were a) trying to retain our employees, and b) find the next good employee (or two) who could lead projects and help grow the business to over twenty people. Learning from experience, I found that every good project leader allowed me to hire an additional five to seven employees to fill that person's projects, so finding that next great leader was very important.

I really didn't know how large we could grow our company, but since we had competitors, plenty of business, and still didn't have contacts with most companies in town, I assumed we could easily get to twenty-plus employees, and as long as we kept hiring good people we wouldn't have to sacrifice quality.

Converted the company to an LLC

I use the word "we" in that last paragraph because by now I had worked with a lawyer to convert the company from an S-Corporation to an LLC, and made several of the most valuable employees *partners* in the business. I still owned the majority of the company, but in working with the lawyer and our accountant, I sold chunks of it to other employees during these years.

I started off selling "shares" in the company, with the shares priced so the partners buying into the company would start to get a return on their investment in twelve months. For example, with fifteen employees, average revenue of $140K per employee, and a 15% Net Income, the company's Net Income equates to $315,000 per year (I document these numbers in Appendix A of this book, "Financial Assumptions"); so, if a partner bought one share, I priced that share at $3,150. With the assumption that our business remained steady, the Net Income corresponding to their share for the next year would match this value, and if business and net income increased their shares would be worth even more.

Over time I gradually increased the price of these shares, but even at these higher prices the new partners were getting their money back quickly with our dividend distributions, and after their first dividend check, no partner ever complained to me about the price of their purchases.

The term "Share" is not correct in an LLC

I'm going to keep using the word "share" throughout this book because it's easier to write, but it's important to note that it isn't technically accurate. In an LLC, nobody owns actual stock, like you do in a Corporation or S-Corporation. Instead, partners own a percentage of the company. While I sold the company in whole numbers that we referred to as shares (i.e., 1% ownership equated to "one share"), you can also sell interest in an LLC in any fraction you want. For instance, I could have sold 0.1% interest in the business if I wanted to.

So, to summarize, whenever I say "share" anywhere in this book, I'm just using that word for convenience, and what I really mean is "1% ownership interest in the company."

Employee ownership and business partners

As a result of my selling interest in the company to people I thought were worthy of being business partners, by the end of the year 2000 the breakdown in ownership looked like this:

- 62% - Me (Class A Partner)
- 20% - Jack (Class A Partner)
- 12% - David (Class A Partner)
- 4% - George (Class B Partner)
- 2% - Cooper (Class B Partner)

I sold interest in the business for two reasons. First, I was -- and still am -- a big believer in employee ownership. I believe that having ownership in a company is a terrific motivator. It helps everyone focus on their work, and what's important in their work. Even in my own case, I know it's helped me get out of bed and into the office on days I didn't feel well. (I share a story later in the diary about how we won a huge deal when Jack told me we'd lose a new account unless I came to a meeting, even though I was in bed with the flu.)

When I first started the company I looked into setting up a formal ESOP, until I realized that an ESOP was primarily a stock ownership structure for larger businesses. After discussing what I wanted with my attorney, he advised me to convert the company to an LLC, so I could sell interest in the company to my key employees, as I've described here.

My second reason for doing this was that in the years prior to 2000, I was competing against "dot-com" companies trying to recruit my employees with lower salaries, but dreams of millions of dollars. I wanted to offer ownership anyway, but this environment really forced the situation.

Class A and B partners

As I showed in that list of employee-owners, two of these co-owners were "Class A" partners, and the other two were "Class B" partners. I used a standard "off the shelf" Operating Agreement from my attorney when I switched the company to an LLC, and with that Agreement, the primary difference between these two levels of partnership is that *Class A* partners have official voting rights, while *Class B* partners do not. If push came to shove, the Class A partners could vote on what to do in a given situation, but as a practical matter I felt like it was important to get everyone's buy-in on major decisions, so we never officially counted votes on any matter; most decisions seemed obvious, so we generally agreed quickly, and moved on.

That being said, to me the Class A partners are truly essential to the business, are actively involved in promoting the business, attending business functions, and helping in sales meetings. The Class B partners, on the other hand, are extremely talented individuals who either don't seem as interested in all aspects of a business, or are newer to the company.

It's important to note that there's another distinction between Class A and Class B partners that didn't seem important at this time. If a problem came up with a Class B partner, I could easily buy back their shares at "book value," and eject them from the company if I wanted to, but getting rid of a Class A partner would be much more difficult. I knew these terms were in the Operating Agreement, but it didn't seem that important back then. Unfortunately, as you'll see from the diary, I should have paid much more attention to this clause.

So much happened in our business in the years 2000 through 2002, I could easily write a separate book about everything we did to survive. If the first few years of business were at the "very easy" end of the spectrum, the years 2000-2002 were way, way over at the "difficult" end.

I'm glad to say we survived the dot-com bust, and then survived the bad business environment that followed September 11, 2001. By mid-2002 I considered us fortunate to still have the same fifteen full-time employees. We didn't have to lay anyone off, and nobody left the company.

But it wasn't all good news. Business did slow down, and it led to some disputes between the partners. If I had written this book back in 2002 I'm sure I would have worded this section more strongly, but in retrospect the best thing to say is that through these difficult years there were a number of disagreements between myself, Jack, and George.

I'll describe some of these disagreements shortly, but right now I'll just ask this question of you: Have you ever had a dispute with someone over a fundamental belief/philosophy that significantly changed your relationship with that person? Perhaps a relative, a spouse, or a good friend?

If so, that's where I was in mid-2002. Ever since the dot-com bust in 2000, I found myself battling against Jack and George about major business and employee decisions, and it had taken it's toll on me, as I'm sure it did on them. At one point it was bad enough that I offered to buy their shares back at the same price I sold to them (even though our income was now reduced), but they didn't take me up on that offer.

(In one of those interesting "timing" events in life, as I edit this section in 2010, I just read an interview about a documentary titled *Once Brothers*. In the interview a basketball player named Vlade Divac says, "To build a friendship takes so much time and so many years. To ruin it, just seconds." So true.)

During these discussions I really began to appreciate David. While I had always liked him before, he was a real calming force during our talks. Like myself, he enjoyed working with everyone at the company, and didn't want to see anyone laid off. Any time the discussions seemed to get out of control, David calmly brought up the financial numbers, and said wise things like, "This is the worst business has ever been, and we're still making a ton of money. What's the problem?"

Death of a friend

In the spring of 2002 a friend of mine named Jim died of a heart attack on the morning of the Kentucky Derby. For ten years running, my wife and I have had a day-long party to celebrate the Derby. Since the Derby is so close to Cinco de Mayo, we combine the two events, placing small bets on the horse races all day while enjoying margaritas and Mexican beer, and grilling fajitas in the evening with a wonderful recipe we learned while living in Texas.

That day we had invited roughly twenty people to the party, but I remember thinking the night before how much fun it would be to have Jim over. He had never been over to the house, and I thought he'd love a good drink and cigar as much as I did. Most of my other friends weren't into sports, but Jim was, so I was looking forward to doing battle with him on the ping-pong table as well. (We had both recently seen the movie *Michael*, and had been yelling "Battle!" a lot lately when goofing around.)

I can't do justice to describing Jim, other than to say that he was all about experiencing life, and you had fun when you were with him. Whether we were working on computers or doing anything else, we made each other laugh. The day before Jim died, we had a salsa-eating contest at a Mexican restaurant, seeing who could eat the hottest salsa mix. Neither of us "won" that contest, but in the midst of a stressful period, it was a lot of fun, and our waitress laughed as much as we did.

All-hands meeting

My main lingering disagreement with Jack and George had to do with an increase in "bench time" for our consultants. If you're not familiar with the consulting world, when consultants don't have a billable project to work on, they're said to be "on the bench." After several years of having nothing but 100% billable employees, we now had several consultants on the bench, and this was a new and frightening experience for all of us, and of course it had a big impact on revenue and profit.

My issue with Jack and George was that they wanted to release the employees who *happened* to be on the bench, while I did not. These were not only our friends, they were also smart, hard-working people -- I would have let them go much earlier if they weren't good employees. The way I looked at it, it wasn't *their* fault they were riding the bench, it was *our* fault for not finding work for them. Jack and George wanted to let them go to keep our profit margins up.

For a long time, I didn't discuss the bench time with our regular employees. The only thing I told them was that in a way it was a welcome situation, and gave us time to write some software for ourselves, mainly to improve our billing software, and also to write a custom content management system for our web hosting clients.

Maybe because he was straddling both sides of the fence, after a while David suggested we (the partners) talk to everyone about the health of the company. Since I kept stressing during our partner meetings that I liked all of our employees, thought they were all very good at what they did, and didn't want to lay anyone off, he suggested I share that message with them. People with free time on their hands could think about a lot of things, he said.

So in the summer of 2002 I made a rare "all hands" speech. I let everyone know that everyone's job was safe at the current work levels. I promised them that if there was a problem they'd hear it from me first, that no such problem existed right now, and I didn't want to lose any of them. I told them that if they enjoyed working with us as well, I didn't want anyone to even think about updating their resumes.

We also asked everyone at the meeting to suggest other ideas on how we could use this bench time. It sounds cliche, but we talked about using this time as an "opportunity" instead of a "problem," and I was glad when they brought up several good ideas, both during and after the meeting. We implemented several of the suggestions, and these changes helped to improve our company in the long run.

Before this experience I had always thought bench time was evil, but at least in this case, I was glad we used the downtime to improve several things at the company we wouldn't have addressed otherwise.

Now that you have this background material, the remainder of this book contains my diary entries related to selling my business.

HOW I SOLD MY BUSINESS

THE DIARY

All of our employees are back to work full-time again, and *now* we're talking about adding a few contractors to handle any extra work that comes up. Such is the life cycle of the consulting business. I'm happy we talked with all the employees this summer about our financial condition, and even happier that nobody left.

I'm sure glad we're not a public company. I'd hate to have a bunch of shareholders harassing me about keeping our profit margin up to a certain level during difficult business times. While they may think that's what they want, this experience reinforced the belief that that's short-term thinking, and it isn't good for long-term business.

If there was anything good about having employees on the bench, it was that it gave us more motivation to go out and sell our services, knowing that we had employees on the bench who could service new accounts immediately. When everyone is billing 100% or more of their time, a consulting firm doesn't have anything to sell (unless you can find more good employees), but when there's bench time we suddenly had a "product" to sell again.

As I think about this, if all I had to do was add new projects without having to worry about hiring great employees to fulfill them, this business would be a breeze. For me, selling a new prospect on our services feels at least 100 times easier than finding great employees.

While the business is in great shape again, I feel completely worn out, and I hope to take a little vacation time soon to recharge the batteries.

My wife and I have been trying to slip in an "emergency" vacation this month, but it's clear now that isn't going to happen. A couple of problems with large clients have come up, and I feel like I need to take care of those personally.

I'm holding out hope that we can at least squeeze in a three-day weekend somewhere nearby. At times like these I really appreciate those "three day vacation" ideas in the local papers and magazines. Of course on one local three-day excursion we ran into a biker's convention, but that ended up being a good time. (Unlike a poor previous manager of mine, who took a short break in Virginia Beach, only to be there for the riots in 1989.)

In happier news, I ran into a potential new project manager when I gave a presentation last Friday. We have some mutual friends, and I've talked to him on and off for two years now, but after the presentation he expressed an interest in interviewing with us, so we're meeting for lunch tomorrow to get the ball rolling.

Argh ... it's been two weeks since my last entry here, and the project manager I've been recruiting for most of the month just turned me down.

I'm upset with him, but really, I'm just upset at our situation. He seemed like the next "technical project manager" I was looking for, and losing him also means losing a chance to hire several new employees that could work with him on projects. We need someone like him to grow the company, and I'm just upset at not being able to hire him, or at least someone like him.

It seems that despite everything we've tried since what -- 1998? -- we've been unable to grow the size of the company. On the one hand I'm glad to still have fifteen employees, but we're just not having any success recruiting the next project leader. I've checked with a variety of friends, and I know that our pay is very competitive, but what we can't offer are "geeky" things like a huge server farm that a techie can play with, or even a regular office they can go to every day.

As consultants, we end up working in whatever situation our clients have set up for us; sometimes that setup is very nice, and other times it's a cubicle in a very loud work area. I've enjoyed some of the crazier setups -- two folding tables with my own Sun servers in a telephone company warehouse, and a similar situation in the basement of a financial business in England -- but cubicles are a big turnoff to techies, and we do have some people working in those right now.

With this person I've been trying to recruit, he told me his biggest hang-up was leaving a multi-million dollar server farm and network setup at his current job. He's worked there ten-plus years, he ordered most of that equipment, and he's comfortable there, while things like working with several clients, more income, and a chance at partnership in the company weren't as strong an appeal for him as managing his current setup. I'm sure the uncertainty in the economy is also an issue for him.

We have three good project managers in the company, including myself, George, and a third person -- Jack's wife -- who is good at running smaller projects, and isn't a partner yet. But as I keep striking out trying to recruit other good project leaders, and other employees don't seem ready to lead anything more than a one- or two-person project, we're stuck. We just can't handle any more business without someone who can lead projects. (We typically service mid-size clients, and they won't pay for a dedicated project manager, so I'm looking for someone who can run a project, and also manage the client relationship.)

More frustrations

Besides being frustrated with this particular hiring issue, I continue to drift apart from Jack, and to some extent George. These are the two guys I've been at odds with during the last few years, and even in this improved business environment, it feels like we can't get past our old disagreements.

I hate to reminisce, but I do miss the old days. When we first started the company everyone did whatever it took to get new customers and generally just get the job done. These days that excitement is gone, and it feels much more like a job: Go in to work, do my time, go home -- and I have to say, that's a sad state for a business owner.

My motivational problem is not being able to grow the company. When we started off we all said we wanted to be "small but good," but staying the same size has become boring. We have great employees, and at this size it's all much easier than I expected it to be, so I'd like to see what it's like to grow the company into something larger.

However, while I've been trying to grow the company, I've felt alone in this effort. I could be wrong, but while I've been trying to expand the business, I feel like the other partners have been pulling back, essentially saying, "We're more comfortable here." For instance, at a two-hour technical seminar we gave recently, Jack left immediately after the start of the seminar, so we didn't have any sales representation during the break or after the seminar, and that's just one example of what I've been running into.

So I feel like I've been beating my head against the wall, or more accurately, it's felt like a tug of war, and at the moment I give up. The way I feel today, if the company is going to grow it's going to have to be because of someone else's effort, or luck, because I seriously need a break.

Taking the advice of my current client who I'm also friends with, I declared today a "Mental Health Day" for myself. I called my client to let them know I wasn't coming in, left a message at the office, had breakfast at my favorite restaurant, and then went to the zoo. For some reason I like to go to the zoo once a year, with or without other people, and I love to commune with the polar bears. Since nobody had called with a dire emergency by the time I got to the zoo, I turned my phone off, and wandered around for a few hours, spending most of the time watching the bears.

In an interesting piece of timing, one of my nieces is planning to get married soon, and I talked to her tonight about love and marriage. We used to have a good relationship, but I haven't spoken to her much in the last few years, until tonight. She seemed very nervous, and asked all sorts of questions. In response, besides asking the obvious questions, such as whether she loved him and trusted him completely, I tried to share some of my recent experiences with her.

I asked if she and her partner have had any major disagreements, and when she replied "Yes," I asked her more questions about how those went. How did he handle the disagreements? Did she feel differently about him after the arguments, or did she still respect him?

Learning about people

Along with my partner issues at work, this conversation reminds me of an experience I had just after high school. I was working at a Kmart, and one Sunday morning they put me back in the garden center with another young girl, and it was one of those "everything that could go wrong went wrong" kind of days. People who were supposed to come in to work didn't show up, whoever worked the night before didn't do their job, and it was a beautiful summer day -- meaning we were swamped with customers. To this day I don't know if I've ever worked as hard as I did that day.

But I learned something about myself that day, and about the girl I worked with. After our initial panic, we kept our attitudes very positive. Instead of bemoaning our fate, we took the day as a challenge. I talked our manager into giving us free soft drinks and lunch, and in exchange we moved customers and product as fast as possible. We smiled, laughed, actively engaged customers, and shared stories during the few quiet moments. We went to high school together for four years but barely said hello to each other then, so it was fun to hear her thoughts about different people in school.

I didn't think about it much back then, but over the years, whenever I look back at that day, I realize that you learn more about people during bad times than you do during easier times. That's one time when a person's true character shows up, and that's what I tried to stress with my niece during our discussion.

Tuesday, October 8, 2002

I came back to the office late this afternoon, greeted all the employees I rarely see because I'm usually not there, settled in to the comfortable old chair behind my desk, and began thumbing through the stack of mail sitting on my desk. I'm often out of the office for days or even weeks at a time working on client projects, and my assistant stacks up anything that looks like junk mail on my desk, and calls or sends an email if anything looks important.

While thumbing through today's stack, I found an envelope from a local business I've never heard of. Opening the letter, I saw it was from someone who calls himself a "business broker," and while it felt like a form letter in many ways, it was also slightly personal. The letter said this broker had someone who might be interested in buying my business.

"Check it out"

A few years ago I would have tossed this letter in the trash without giving it a second thought, but with my feeling of being "stuck" at our current employment level, my feeling that Jack, George, and I aren't on the same page any more, plus a little burnout, I put the letter on the side, and then kept looking back at it as I worked through the rest of the mail.

It was now late in the day, and all my co-workers had gone home, except for my wife, who takes care of the books and many other things at the company. When my schedule opened up this afternoon so I could swing by the office, we made plans for a 6:30 dinner.

I buried the letter in the small stack of mail I was keeping, looked out into the parking lot, saw that all the employee's cars were gone, then walked through the office just to make sure nobody else was there. When I found my wife, I showed her the letter, and asked what she thought. "Check it out" was pretty much all she said. We try not to talk about work much at home, but she knows I haven't been happy with many things about work lately, and I think she just wants me (us) to be happy.

After discussing the letter with my wife a couple of days ago, I put it in my computer bad, and I've found myself glancing at it several times lately. The conversation in my head was something like this: "Is it a form letter? Yes, it almost surely was, but he does state he has a potential buyer. He'd have to be a scumbag to send something like this out if he doesn't really have a potential buyer."

Today I finally showed it to Jack, and asked what he thought. Without any hesitation he said, "Let's check it out." I took his immediate response as a sign that he was as tired of fighting with me as I was with him about the future of the company.

Later this afternoon we showed the letter to David, and while he wasn't excited about it, he said it sounded interesting, especially if he was going to get "a big barrel of money." However, he added that he wasn't anywhere near being ready to retire yet, and needed to work for many more years, and wanted to make sure he'd have a good job after the sale. Other than that, he said he'd support us in whatever we wanted to do.

Although the Class B partners will soon be Class A partners, they don't technically have a say in how the business is run, so we didn't bother to run this by them yet. I also got guarantees from Jack and David that despite their friendships with the other partners, we would only talk to them about this if something interesting came up. I also told my wife she couldn't discuss this with anyone, not Jack, David, or anyone else. After all, it's very possible nothing at all will happen, and things will go back to the way they were a few days ago.

Calling the business broker

Late this afternoon I called this business broker from my home, told him I received his letter, and grilled him as much as I could over the phone. I'm easily turned off by most salespeople, and assumed this conversation would be over quickly, but to my pleasant surprise, the broker, a man named Marty, spoke in a very straightforward manner. Yes, he did have a prospective buyer, two actually, though he didn't know enough about their financial situations yet.

Not turned off by him immediately, I set up a meeting for the following week. He suggested that we meet at his office, and specifically not meet at our office or even in public. He said it would be much easier to have our conversation without having to worry about anyone that might be within earshot. I agreed to this, and told him I didn't know who might come to the meeting with me, but he should expect two or three people.

Marty's office is in a nice part of town, and it's not near any of our customer sites, and to the best of my knowledge, it's also not near any of our employee's homes. To my further relief, I found that his office was in the back of a small business complex, one of those office areas with rows of one-story buildings, with about six or eight offices per building, and his office was near the end of the last strip facing a small forested area. From here it would have been nearly impossible for anyone to see me park my car and walk into the office of a business broker. If I didn't feel like I was sneaking around earlier today when I decided not to wear any of our company logo wear, I definitely felt like it now.

David didn't want to come to the meeting, so Jack met me in the parking lot, and we walked into Marty's office together. I've walked into hundreds of offices in my consulting career, but for the first time since I went to see a prospect in a bad neighborhood of our city, I began wondering what I was getting myself into. "Don't worry," I kept telling myself, "you're the customer this time, and if you don't like it, you can just say you're not interested, and walk away."

I go by instinct a lot when I first meet people, and during this meeting I came to like Marty. We met for nearly three hours, and I didn't see or hear anything to make me distrust him. A simple description of him is that he reminded me of a prototypical southern gentleman, and he also reminded me of my first boss out of college, which is a positive comparison. I'll guess his age is somewhere in his upper fifties or low sixties.

His office is very conservative, and although he mentioned that he had a part-time secretary, she wasn't there this afternoon. While our office is overflowing with computers and computer parts wherever you look, he had two computers visible in his *entire* office, an old PC on his desk, and another one for his secretary. I just happened to watch an old *Columbo* episode from the 1970s last night, and his office reminded me of a scene in an office where Columbo saw a fax machine for the first time.

Marty began the meeting much the same way Jack and I normally begin a meeting with a new prospect, giving us a little bit of literature and a brief history of his company. While our literature consists of glossy, full-color pages printed on a $2,500 printer, Marty's literature was a short two-page document, with plain text printed on standard white paper, basically a resume, detailing his business experiences.

He started his own company, sold it, and then bought it back when things went bad for the new owners. He built it back up again, and (amazingly and amusingly) sold it back to the same people.

Still longing for something to do after selling his business twice, he became involved in two other businesses, eventually helping to sell them. After that he realized he had stumbled into a career he enjoyed, and he set up shop as a business broker. Since then, he's been involved in eighteen business transactions, and gave us several references to call.

Marty next handed us a document, which turned out to be a very simple non-disclosure agreement. To my surprise, it's nothing for *us* to sign. It's a document that says that even in this preliminary "exploratory" stage, he won't disclose anything we talk about here today. He signed this document, made a copy of it on a modern, multi-purpose copier/printer/fax machine, and gave us the original.

Financial information about our business

Next, Marty told us we didn't have to give him any exact numbers, but he would like ballpark numbers about our business, including revenue, profit, how many employees we have, etc. At this point I was very suspicious, and despite his NDA, I didn't feel comfortable sharing this much information. Rather than dance around the issue, I just told him that.

To help me relax, Marty turned to his computer, typed something in, and then proceeded to tell us all about the financials of our company. When the information he told us sounded extremely accurate, I asked him how he got it. He invited us to come over and look at his computer monitor, where I saw an old DOS-based application with very accurate financial details about our company. I have no idea how long I stared at it, but it was right. We don't share our financial information with anyone, so I was stunned to see it on his screen.

I asked Marty where he got it, and he said it was standard software in his business. (I'm writing this diary many months after the actual event, and unfortunately I don't remember the name of this software, but I'll guess it's related to Dun & Bradstreet, Risk Management Associates, Hoovers, or a similar firm.) He said all of this information was culled together from various tax and business filings, and that he didn't know how it worked, but it always seemed accurate. Indeed it was, shockingly accurate.

Seeing that he already had access to so much information about our business, I opened up and gave him other ballpark information about number of employees, revenue, and net income. He asked for some other information, and while I can't remember what else he asked, I remember thinking there was no reason for him to know this information yet, so I politely declined. He said that was okay, but if we were going to take the steps to sell our business, he would need that information eventually.

Next, Marty caught me by surprise, and asked why we want to sell our business. (Oops, I thought, I hadn't prepared for that question at all.) With his question, Marty said that if the business financials we were looking at were real, our business sounded like a genuine goldmine, and he's surprised we would want to sell it.

I told Marty that you had to temper some of the profit numbers by knowing that most of the business partner's spouses are involved in the business, and they're providing some services much cheaper than the going rate. A couple of the partner's base salaries are a little low, which also increases net income.

But beyond that, I told Marty the truth about my frustration in trying to grow the business, and how the projects I work on force me to be out of the office most of the time, keeping me from doing some of the things I really enjoy doing. I also told him his letter caught me at a time when I was tired, and probably need a long vacation.

After I finished, Jack told a similar story, in particular saying that his role at the company isn't what he originally expected, and he has his own frustrations, also not getting to do some of the things he enjoys. If nothing else, it was interesting to hear his side of the story, sort of a business partner therapy. At least one thing we have in common is that the demands of the company have taken us away from the things we most enjoy.

At this point I qualified some of what I said, telling Marty that I would be interested in staying with the company after a sale. I told him that if I could just keep work under sixty hours a week, and if the company were growing and interesting, I could probably be a software consultant and business owner for a very long time.

The next step

After this, Marty told us that the next step in the process was for him to work up a "valuation" of our company, and to do that he was going to need our P&L and Balance Sheet statements for the last three years. He also wanted some other information about any recurring revenue we might have, customers under long-term contracts, information about debt, liabilities, lawsuits, and anything else that would impact the value of our company one way or another.

If we could provide him with all that information, he'd work up an estimate of what he thinks our business is worth, and we can make a "yes" or "no" decision about putting the business up for sale after that.

(I didn't know it then, but I now know that all of this is standard information that any business broker will need.)

Potential business buyers

We asked Marty several times during the conversation if he did know any potential buyers, and he kept saying yes, but asked us to be patient as we answered all of his questions. By now we were into the third hour of our meeting, and were finally getting back to this point.

Marty told us he did have two possible buyers, and one was an individual, and the other was another local computer services business. But he also cautioned that while these people do seem interested in buying a computer programming and web design business like ours, we shouldn't get our hopes up, that most deals fall through, and we need to be prepared for the long haul. He told us that he's never been involved in a sale that went to the first prospective buyer. Buying a business, he told us, takes a lot of time and research, as well as a good match between the buyer and seller.

As for his pay, Marty told us that he wouldn't ask us for any money up front, and in fact, we shouldn't trust any business broker who asks to be paid that way. He would make his income as a commission during the sales process, and his rate was 10%, and it wasn't negotiable. To be very clear, he said that if the business sold for $2M, his commission would be $200K, and that amount would have to be paid at closing time, regardless of our terms with the buyer.

(I would later learn that this is a common commission rate for a business broker. In fact, I've learned that brokers typically charge commissions according to a Lehman formula, essentially charging a higher commission for smaller sales, and a lower rate for larger sales.)

If I didn't feel this way already, by now the thought of selling my business felt a lot like selling a house, with a few key distinctions. First, I've never built a house, but I did build this business, and now we were talking about it like this tangible "thing" that could be bought. I'd never thought of my business as something to be sold, but I also never really thought of it as "my baby" -- at least not until now. While my curiosity was piqued, this thought of "selling my baby" was making me feel a little sick. I kept thinking, "Do I really want to do this?"

Second, Marty mentioned that he won't mind if we say "no" to any buyers that we don't like, but that he'd be really disappointed if we backed out of a deal where all the terms were good, and we liked the other party, but just had a change of heart. He suggested that if we think we might have a change of heart we shouldn't even start this process, because it would be a waste of time for everyone.

(This gave me a flashback of a discussion I had with a monk at a Zen monastery many years ago. For years I had thoughts that perhaps I should be a Zen monk, so during one visit I asked a Zen

Master how I should know if I should be a monk or not. He said that if I had just a 1% thought that I didn't want to be a monk, then I shouldn't be one. Since I have "attachments" to things like margaritas, I decided to be a businessman who practices Zen, instead of a monk.)

As the meeting ended, Marty gave us a small packet of forms that we'd need to fill out if we decided to go down this road of trying to sell our business with him.

After the meeting

After the meeting Jack and I leaned on our cars in Marty's parking lot for at least fifteen minutes, even saying goodnight to Marty as he went home, as it was now well after dinner time. We both felt like Marty was trustworthy, and we talked about what it felt like to think of selling "our baby," with a few comments about how neither one of us was doing exactly what we wanted to be doing.

We agreed to think about this as long as we needed to, to make sure we wouldn't feel like backing out later. When I got home I told my wife the pertinent details of the meeting, telling her I thought Marty was okay, and that Jack and I were thinking about it. I told her that if we went forward it looked like we'd have to put together a lot of financial information, and she would be responsible for putting together most of it.

After getting tied up in regular business matters for several days, Jack and I finally had lunch together today, and agreed that we wanted to explore selling the business. We had no idea what the company was worth, but we wanted to take the next step to find out. We called David to tell him we wanted to do it, but he was at a client site and couldn't say much more than "okay."

It felt weird, but in the middle of this little hole-in-the-wall restaurant that we like, we started working on some of the business documents Marty had given us. After lunch I called Marty from the car and told him we wanted to take the next step with him, to find out how much the business was worth. I told him we had started to work on the documents he gave us, and he told me to just drop off all the documents when they were ready.

If I was looking for something interesting and exciting to recharge my batteries, I've found that. I'm not really thinking about leaving the company so much as I am thinking about finding someone to grow the company with, maybe someone who can help Jack and I get back to doing what we like.

While it's exciting, it's also nerve-wracking, because every time I open my mouth I have to think about who I'm talking to. I can't tell anyone else about this, but I'm excited about it, and I wish I could.

SATURDAY, OCTOBER 19, 2002

David and I were both at the office for a while this morning (a Saturday morning), and we spent a little time talking about the business broker. He asked how the meeting went with the guy, what he was like, what he wanted, how he'd be paid, etc. He reiterated that he was okay with this if it was something I wanted to do, and he just wanted his big, fat buyout and a good-paying job when it was all over.

As we spoke, the topic of the Class B partners came up. Since we were alone at the office, we decided to get Jack on a quick conference call, and the three of us agreed not to talk to the Class B partners about this yet, as we still didn't have any idea what our company was worth. If the business broker said the company wasn't worth much, we might still decide not to sell the business, and we didn't see any sense in worrying the Class B partners about this yet.

Wow, I can see how getting financial information together for a business broker could be a real problem at many companies. The list is very detailed, and includes:

- Business P&L statements for the last three years.
- Balance sheets for the last three years.
- Income and length of engagement with all of our major customers. He doesn't need customer names, and said we should whiteout all the names, changing them to Customer A, Customer B, etc.
- A business organizational chart. This was the first laugh Jack and I had together in a long time. An org chart, at our company? Really?
- Key employees and job descriptions.
- Three pages of other questions related to how we ran the business. This is all basic business and financial information (I'll list some questions shortly), but it's going to take a while to put it together. I started to think that some of this was just a ruse to see if we are truly committed to this process, but I called Marty, and he told me it's all needed for potential buyers. He doesn't need to see all of it right now for his needs, but potential buyers will need it. He said to skip anything we don't feel comfortable with, but he will definitely need the P&L and Balance Sheet information.

As I started to write, for many small business getting this financial information together would be a real issue. Think about it: This information is going to take someone at least a few days to put together, and at the very least, your bookkeeper and/or accountant will have to be involved in the process.

Preparing the financial information

Fortunately my wife oversees the bookkeeping portion of the business, so we just took a recent backup copy of the financial server and set up a computer for her at home. I handle the backups of the financial server, so again, this is easily done.

With my wife getting all the financial information together offsite, Jack and I met several times to answer the other questions, things like:

- What was our marketing budget and marketing strategy?
- What is the average length of a customer engagement?
- Who are our biggest customers, how long have we been working with them, and how long did we expect these relationships to last?
- List any long-term contracts we had with customers. Marty told us during our meeting that buyers love to see customers signed to long-term contracts and recurring revenue.
- Describe our history of employee turnover.
- Who are the key employees? What do they do?
- Would we stay after the sale? If so, how long?
- Many more ...

Again, Jack and I didn't see the rationale behind several of these right now, so we just put "Later" on the response we were preparing. One example is where we didn't think the names of any employees needed to be shared at this time, especially when we had no idea what the company was worth.

Marty's list also includes two other items that are very interesting:

- The names of all companies Marty should *never* contact about selling our business.
- The names of any companies that we recommend Marty contacting to see if they would be interested in buying a business like ours.

Marty mentioned these points before, but I had forgotten about them. In regards to the second list, he did mention to us earlier that any companies he contacted would only see "blinded" information, i.e., basic financial information about our company, including a generic profile, including approximate number of employees, and that we are a computer consulting firm. But there would be no names, and no exact physical location, just that this is "a software consulting company located in the Midwest."

Between my wife, myself, and Jack, we were able to put all this research together without involving anyone else at the company. Since we already had our regular day jobs, putting it all together took almost two weeks. Once we knew we'd be done by a certain date, I called Marty and set up an appointment for the following week.

It's probably helpful to share some financial information about our company here. To keep everyone's information private, and to make this easier, I've gone through this entire book and changed all the financial values, including things like Revenue, Net Income ratio, and actual Net Income. I've documented my approach in Appendix A (Financial Assumptions), but as a quick summary:

- We have fifteen employees.
- Based on my research, a typical computer consulting firm earns $140K per employee.
- Multiply those numbers and you get a yearly revenue of $2.1M.
- A typical computer consulting firm has a Net Income ratio of 15%.
- Using that ratio, our Net Income would be $315,000 per year.

Like other LLCs I know, we also have partner distributions at least twice a year. As mentioned earlier, if a partner owns 10% of the company, a simple way to look at it is that $31,500 would go into their capital account. I discuss *capital accounts* in detail later, so I'll leave this discussion here at this time.

FRIDAY, OCTOBER 25, 2002

I planned to just drop off all the paperwork with Marty, but on our last call he suggested that Jack and I drop it off together, and plan to stay a little while as he reviewed it.

At his office, we gave Marty all of the information we had put together. He gave it a preliminary review, asking a few questions as he looked it over, and scribbled something about our responses. As he reviewed it, we reiterated our concerns about answering some of the questions, and he said that was fine for now, but he would need it later if we decided to move forward. This review process took about ninety minutes, and I was glad Jack came to help with a few of the questions.

At the conclusion of the meeting Marty said the next step was for him to work up his appraisal of our company's value, after which he would present his "business valuation." He mentioned that he would create his business valuation using a "cash flow" method, but he didn't provide any more details about his approach. Because of his schedule, he said this would take almost two weeks before he could be ready, and we set a date to meet again.

Books on selling a business and business valuations

I had already started reading some information on business valuations, mostly on the internet, but I decided that while Marty was working up his appraisal, I was going to the bookstore to find whatever information I could about the process of selling a business, specifically how to value a company. However, on the drive to the bookstore, I decided it wouldn't be a good idea to run into any employees or customers while I was standing in the "How to sell your business" section, so I decided to rush-order several books from Amazon instead.

THURSDAY, NOVEMBER 7, 2002

Two weeks have come and gone since my last entry, and I have to admit, it's been an anxious time. Besides pretending to be a normal small business owner, I've been coming home most nights and tried to digest these "How to buy/sell a business" books. I've tried to do my homework, working through several valuation examples, but the array of business valuation formulas is very confusing.

Based on the valuation formulas and rudimentary examples found in four different books, it looks like our company is worth anywhere between $315K and $5M. As you might guess, that isn't very helpful.

Business valuation methods

It turns out there a lot of different ways to value businesses, including:

- Book Value Method
- Multiples of Revenue
- Capitalization of Earnings Method
- Continuing Value Method
- The Excess Earnings Method
- The Asset Value Method

There are even more business valuation methods than these, but these are the ones I see repeated in the four books I have, and in the other research I've done on the internet.

Trying my own business valuation

With our business being a service-oriented business -- and with me being more of an engineer and less of a financial person -- the only business valuation approach that make sense to me is:

- Try to determine the net income from ongoing operations.
- Make some assumptions about how the company would change after the sale.

- Make some assumptions about business revenue after the sale.
- Try to determine the income to the new owners of the business.

Without using any specific method, I know that with our current situation, our net income has averaged $315K per year lately. I have to think the overall company is easily worth that, or even twice that ($630K). This has to be tempered by the fact that many of our employee-owners will want raises if they sell their interest, but still, it's a place to start.

Some of the techniques show that our company may be worth as much as $5M, though I don't understand how that can be possible. Taking the rough middle ground between a low of $315K and a high of $5M, another guess is that our company may be worth $2.5M, though I'm not at all confident in that number.

I have to say, it's a good feeling to think that you've created a company out of thin air, and a decade later this company may be worth $2.5M. It isn't a huge fortune, but hey, it's something.

As I read all these books and go back over Marty's paperwork, it's interesting to learn that there is a profession known as "business valuators," people who are hired to determine the value of a business. I knew a little bit about this before, especially because our Operating Agreement has a clause in it that "a business valuator may be used in the event of a partner separating from the business," but I didn't create this business with the idea of selling it one day, so it wasn't anything I gave a lot of thought to. (Frankly, I don't know exactly why I created this business, other than my inability to be satisfied working for other people.)

Discounted future cash flows

As a final note here tonight, I keep reading about "discounted future cash flows." This is a new term to me (which shows how much of a novice I am about business financials), so I thought I better research it.

The basic premise goes like this: Assuming there is inflation, a dollar you hold in your hand isn't going to be worth as much in the future. Using an example inflation rate of 4% annually, right now a dollar is worth 100 cents; in a year it will be worth 96 cents; in two years it will be worth roughly 92 cents, and so on. There's more to it than this, but I think that's the basic idea behind it.

I was just reminded of this again as I was working through one of these book examples, and ran across this quote:

"The theory behind discounting future cash or cash equivalents to a present value is that a dollar received today is worth more than a dollar to be received in the future."

This isn't a big deal to me right now, but it looks like something a business valuator needs to consider when looking at a projected future income for a business, especially if payouts are made over several years.

Jack and I met at Marty's office today, and I was shocked at the result. Marty gave us a brief introduction into how he appraised our company, and based on his cash flow method, he said our company was worth $5.4M, maybe more.

What followed was truly funny.

Jack and I spent the next two hours telling Marty how he was wrong, that our company couldn't possibly be worth $5.4M. We dug into his numbers, questioned everything, said we thought he was wrong here, here, and here, and in particular we thought he didn't account enough for the replacement costs of the spouses in the business, or the current owner-employees wanting raises if they sold their interest.

Five year break-even

But those were relatively small details. The big number we really didn't agree with is that Marty's assumption was that a buyer would want to break even on the deal in five years. While this might be true in many old-school businesses -- and I saw this in the business valuation books I bought -- the computer industry moves very fast, and I didn't believe anyone would be patient enough to wait that long to break even on a deal. Personally, I can't imagine buying another computer business without breaking even in eighteen months, maybe twenty-four months, tops, and that would be a very nervous twenty-four months.

In the computer industry, everyone's job skills change very significantly every two to four years. A good example of this was an industry referred to as "Novell network resellers" in the 1990s. In the early 1990s, Novell was *the* company to go to when you wanted to build a computer network. But in the mid-1990s when networking became ubiquitous, and Microsoft's networking software became "good enough," many Novell resellers were suddenly worthless, or nearly worthless. If they didn't make the change to use Microsoft's technologies, and open their businesses to new areas like network security, these companies faded off into the sunset. So, a Novell reseller that was worth $2M in 1995 was essentially worthless in 1997 if they didn't change, and that change would cost a lot of money.

So, when Marty was talking about a buyer looking for a five-year payback, I told him no way, that we needed to look at two years tops for a buyer like myself, or maybe three years for someone willing to take a bigger risk.

The meeting ended with Jack and I thinking that nobody would buy the company on anything longer than a buyout term of three years. As mentioned, I personally couldn't imagine a buyout term of more than eighteen to twenty-four months, and thinking of that Novell example, I'd even want something closer to twelve months. With Marty's business valuation working out to roughly $1.1M per year, I was now thinking the company was worth $1.1M to $1.6M (ballpark), while Jack was thinking more in the two to three year range, or $2.2M to $3.3M.

At the end of the meeting Marty told us to review his valuation, and to let him know if we were interested in really selling the company at the prices we were talking about. If and when we were ready to sell the company we'd have to sign some more paperwork authorizing him to be our salesperson, again not unlike working with a realtor to sell a house. He reiterated that he would want a two-year contract and a 10% commission, and those terms weren't negotiable.

Discussing the business valuation

After the meeting at Marty's office, Jack and I drove to a nearby restaurant to try to absorb Marty's calculations.

I couldn't figure out how he was saying that our business was worth $1.1M/year to potential buyers. Even with several spouses working at the company, our net income was still just $315K per year. Sure, one of the new owners might replace Jack or myself, or perhaps both of us, so they would also get our salaries, but that still didn't add up to $1.1M. We also had no idea who the future buyers might be, so it seemed too early to make any guesses there. We'd have to take that on a case-by-case basis.

By the end of my meeting with Jack, we agreed to simplify things and try to imagine selling the business for $2M, with the question being, "Are we willing to sell for $2M?"

I didn't have to think about it too hard; with my ownership stake I knew I was willing to sell at that price, but I had to think about everyone else. The company was only going to be worth this much if everyone agreed to stay at the company and keep working after the sale, and if some key employees wouldn't do this, we'd have a problem selling the business.

Jack had to meet his wife somewhere, so we ran out of time to discuss this any further tonight, but we knew we'd need to discuss this more, and also need to include David in the discussion. If we go forward, we'll have to decide whether we should say anything to the Class B partners, or not.

As I've dug more into Marty's approach, it looks like he's using a "discretionary cash flow" process for his business valuation. This technique assumes that all money the business owners take out of the business -- both normal paycheck income and profit from the business -- is discretionary. As mentioned, on top of that he assumed that a buyer would be looking for a break-even point in five years.

Based on the business valuation books I bought, I had started on this technique myself, but wasn't confident in my approach. But based on his example I reworked my earlier valuation, with a few changes. The first change I made was to assume that we would all stay with the business after a sale, but that we would all need some form of raise to our base salaries to stay with the new owners. There was no exact way to do this, so I made assumptions about what I thought it would take to keep each of the current partners.

Using that as my base spreadsheet, I created several variations from it, assuming the new owners would either replace Jack, myself, or both of us. This may not sound like much, but (for example), if we're both drawing $100K salaries immediately after the sale, and we leave the company after twelve months, and the new owners are looking to break even in 36 months, a simple change like that can mean a $400K difference in business value. ($200K in salary to us during Year 1, then not paying us this $400K in salary during the last twenty-four months.)

Based on all these spreadsheet permutations, I'm comfortable thinking that our business is worth $1.6M to $2.8M, depending on the assumptions used, and the buyout period. Those assumptions will vary with prospective buyers, so at this point, I can't think of any other permutations to run until we meet some buyers and know what they want.

Other thoughts

In addition to all those spreadsheets, there are several other thoughts rumbling around in my head today:

- I'm curious to know if Marty intentionally high-balled us with his $5.4M number, but I'll save that question for another time. The important part is that he did a lot of work for us, and helped us see how a business buyer might value our business.

- In the books that I've read and from what Marty told us, the partners would probably have to stay at the company at least 12-18 months after the sale. This seems especially important in a service business where your work is you, and people are buying into you -- they're trusting you -- so if we were going to leave after the sale we'd have to wean customers off of "us" and onto the new business buyers.

- Marty said that it would be helpful if we could get more of our customers to commit to long-term contracts. For a long time we've just had standing agreements with our customers that we'll do certain things for them, and charge them certain rates, but Marty said that potential business buyers will feel much more comfortable seeing these customers signed up for at least a year or more into the future, even if we have worked with them already for five years or more.

- For Marty to put these spreadsheets together, he didn't really need all those documents we put together. He really just needed the P&L statements and balance sheets for the last few years. I think he put us through those hoops either to make sure we were being honest in what we were saying, or to get us to start buying into the process of selling the company. He knew it would take us a long time to put that information together, so it would be an investment on our part. But thinking purely in inputs and outputs, he just needed our P&L statements and balance sheets to create his spreadsheets.

Sales agent for two years

One thing we discussed at length yesterday is that Marty wants a contract that would make him our "sales agent" for two years. He hasn't asked us for any money, and only gets paid on his commission if we sell our company, so I understand his concern, but two years strikes me as a long-term deal, especially if he really has two potential buyers in his pocket.

Marty explained his side of the story, saying that if these initial deals don't work out, as he's already warned is very possible, that he's going to have spend a fair amount of money and effort advertising our business.

I'm not thrilled with this long-term commitment, but he's told us about it from day one, and I've also seen it in all the books I've read, so it's not a big surprise ... I just don't like it. I'm also excited by the prospect of selling the business at the financial values I've cranked out, let alone the valuation he came up with.

Beyond that, the most important part is that Marty seems trustworthy. I've put him through a lot of paces by now, and he's responded well to everything I've thrown at him. The worst case scenario with him seems to be that nothing happens, we don't sell the company in two years, and we move on, and I can live with that.

As a final note, Jack sent me an email this evening to let me know that he's okay with pursuing selling the business. Next up, we need to talk to David.

Jack and I exchanged some brief emails with David on Sunday, telling him that we wanted to meet with him. With everyone anxious about the process, we had all worked up valuations of some form or another, and the three of us met at my house for lunch today to discuss them.

My valuation efforts sounded more detailed than theirs, so I made photocopies of both Marty's valuation and copies of my best spreadsheets, and presented everything as well as I understood it. David and Jack agreed with some of my assumptions and disagreed with some others, but we were all more or less in the same ballpark.

The most important part of our meeting was that we all agreed we wanted to pursue this. For me, this was the most interesting thing to happen with the company in a while, and it has revived my spirits. Jack and David didn't say anything specifically to this point, but I'll say that they were both deeply involved and curious about the entire process.

Beyond that excitement, the second-most interesting part of the meeting was our discussion about our Class B partners, with the questions being:

- Should we tell the Class B partners what we're doing?
- If so, when should we tell them? Do it now, before we sign Marty's papers? Right when we're ready to sell to an actual party? Or some time in between?

We debated a number of approaches, but we decided to tell the Class B partners immediately, for the following reasons:

- We're thinking about converting George and Cooper to Class A partners very soon.
- We want them to trust us, and putting the company for sale without telling them would be a big blow to this trust.
- We need their buy-in on selling the business. If they weren't willing to stay with the company after the sale, the company would be worth significantly less.

- If the company is really worth $2M, each of their shares in the company would be worth $20K. I hoped they would see this as a nice payback on their investments in the company.

Having agreed on this, we just had to figure out a time to tell them. I didn't want to make it on a weekend, because they would have to tell their spouses they "had to go into work" on a Saturday, and I assumed their spouses would ask more questions about why they had to go in. We agreed to make it seem like a more casual meeting, so I sent out an email tonight to see what afternoon they could meet this week.

We met with all the Class B partners at the office after 5 p.m. today, making sure everyone else was out of the building before we began the meeting. We told them the truth, that we investigated the business sales process out of curiosity after receiving a letter, and brought them all the way up to where we are now.

Initially the Class B partners seemed to be in shock, but once they had a chance to catch their breath they seemed much better. I'll guess that knowing their shares might now be worth $20K each helped calm their nerves.

Without question, the most frequently asked question at the meeting was, "Why are you considering doing this?" I told them that from my part the business had become stale, that I had been trying to grow it forever, and I was frustrated at not being able to do so. I told them I had no idea how things might work out, but if the choice was between staying at the same size for a few more years versus selling to a larger company, or merging with some other company to get larger, those things were more interesting to me now.

In the end the Class B partners may not have been too excited by my motivations, but they agreed the company felt a little stale. Fourteen of the fifteen employees have probably been with us for over five years now, and without growing or doing something different, it seemed like the phrase "same thing, different day" applied to our company.

Although I told the Class B partners they should think about this overnight, or even for a few days, they said that we should go ahead and pursue this. They said it wouldn't help with the general staleness problem at the company, but it would certainly be something interesting for all the partners, assuming we kept them in the loop, which we promised to do.

They also added two other concerns. First, they said that if this got out publicly it would be disastrous for the company, so they agreed that Rule #1 was that this had to be a total, complete secret. This could not be discussed with any family members or friends, period.

Second, they shared the same concern David had much earlier: They would still need a job after the sale, and wanted to make sure they were still welcome to work at whatever the new company was, and in their words, they "didn't want to work for any assholes." I told them I didn't think we'd have any problems there, and also assured them that if something did happen after the sale, they certainly had my recommendation if they needed to go to work somewhere else.

With this behind us, the next step is to sign Marty's paperwork and learn about his prospects.

I had a few phone calls with Jack and David yesterday, and we decided to tell Marty up front that we wouldn't accept a sales price of less than $2M, though of course the more we could get, the better. So I called Marty yesterday and told him that, and he said that was good to know, but he still wanted to price the company higher. He didn't buy into the company being paid back in two years, and thought three years or more was reasonable, and he would use that approach in his discussions with prospects. As a result, I assumed this meant he'd be telling his prospects our company was worth at least $3.3M.

Once we worked through that, he said he'd like to come to our office to sign the paperwork. He wanted to see what the office was like, and see some of the employees for himself. He explained that this would help make his sales process better, and that he'd like to be able to describe the office and environment to his prospects.

As I paused to think about it, he asked me to put myself in his shoes, and imagine I was talking to a prospect about selling the business, and wouldn't I want to know what I was talking about if I was in his shoes?

I agreed that this was a good idea, so he came into the office today, and we gave him the tour we usually give to our prospects. When we meet with new prospects we walk through the office and point out a few key sales points here and there, and this seems to give prospects a better feeling about our company.

Everything went well, but I was holding my breath that one of the employees would see him and say, "Uncle Marty, what are you doing here? Aren't you a business broker?"

Signing the paperwork

After the tour we talked in our conference room. This part was even more awkward than the tour, because the office walls are very thin. Fortunately the conference room isn't too close to anyone's office, except for one dedicated salesperson we have, and fortunately he was out of the office this afternoon.

Before we signed all the paperwork, Marty again assured us that he'll be discreet with our information, and he won't send out any information we don't agree to share. Everything will be "blinded," and his description of our company will be vague, something just a little more detailed than "small, profitable computer software firm in the Midwest."

At this point, this really does feel almost exactly like putting a house up for sale, except the meeting doesn't end with the broker putting a sign up in your front yard, and you also can't tell anyone what you're doing. Marty reminded us again about that part, telling us that it's very dangerous for our employees to find out the business is for sale. If they do, they'll all assume the worst, and start sending their resumes out.

We showed Marty out like we would any other prospect, and I left the office just after him. Frankly, I was having a severe case of feeling guilty, and I didn't want anyone asking me who this prospect was.

As I write these notes tonight, I'm reminded how much easier this process is when the bookkeeper is in on the deal. If the bookkeeper isn't a business partner, or in this case my wife, the business partners would have to do a lot of this work ourselves, without her knowledge. Because I have direct access to the computer backups and I'm very familiar with Quickbooks, I could personally do all of this, but it would take a lot of my personal time, and I appreciate not having to do that.

We didn't take the time to learn about Marty's two prospects today. We were all a little short on time, but we promised to meet again soon to learn more about them.

In retrospect, I'm not sure it was a good idea to give Marty our minimum price. He may tell this number to prospects right away, and if there's one thing I've learned in business, it's that everyone wants a deal. Even when our paperwork is very standard, it's very rare for a prospect to just read it and sign it; it seems like everyone wants a discount, or a little something special added to the deal. We do discount some of our hosting setup fees from time to time, but in the same way that Marty won't negotiate his commission, I never negotiate a billing rate on our consulting deals. To me, discounts are for things like computer hardware and "fees."

Blah, I'm not sure why I'm really worrying about this. Marty seems smart, he's done this before, he wants $3M or more, and he's paid on commission, so the more we get, the more he gets.

In the end, I need to trust him, and I don't think this will be a problem. If anything, I'm more concerned that he'll scare off most buyers by quoting the $5M price. It's a big come down from $5M to $2M, and if a business broker told me a company our size was worth $5M with an earn-back over five years, I wouldn't even bother investigating the deal ... and that really does concern me.

True to his word, Marty has a prospective buyer for our company. Jack and I met with them over breakfast this morning at a restaurant near Marty's office.

I kept second-guessing myself and didn't sleep well last night, but our meeting was surprisingly relaxed and informal. The potential buyer's name is Rob, and I'm surprised to learn that he more or less does what we do here in town. I thought I knew most of our competitors, but I've never heard his name before.

Rob is trying to build his own business, and has several people working with him on a part-time basis, and now that he's comfortable with the consulting business and local industry, he wants to take the next step. Rob is younger than all of us, in his late twenties or possibly early thirties, and seems very aggressive, reminding me of myself at that age. (I'm currently 41 years old, and Jack is about ten years older than I am.)

His revenue numbers pale compared to ours, and I started to think that if things don't work out we should consider buying his business. When we asked about how he would be able to afford to buy our company, he told us that he knows several influential people in town who are willing to back him, and he thinks he can raise enough. Marty vouches for him, saying that he knows the people Rob has been talking with, and he thinks it's possible.

The next step

The meeting went so well that by the end of the breakfast, as we discussed several different ideas about where to go from here, Rob mentioned that he's supposed to meet with a new prospect in the next week or two, and asked if he and I could make the sales call together. He said the prospect was small, and there wasn't a chance for a great deal of revenue, but it would be nice to test our ability to work together. Rob would like to take the sales lead during the meeting, and let me handle all the technical issues. He wants to keep my company name out of the discussion, unless something comes up where we have to mention it.

I told Rob that I'm reasonably well known in town, I've been to a ton of local business events, and my picture has been in the local business newspaper several times, so if someone says they know me, we need to be ready to say that we're looking at partnering on this deal. Although I have some reservations about doing this, it also sounds interesting, so I'm okay with the idea.

I asked Jack what he thought about the idea, and he seemed okay with it, but was concerned about the specifics of how we'd handle it. He reiterated that Rob needed to drop back and tell the truth if the customer recognized me.

Personally, I really liked Rob, and I wanted to explore what it's like to work with him. Again, if he can't raise the money to buy our company, I like the idea of buying his business, hiring his people, and going from there. I get the idea he prefers the sales process, but if he's willing to run projects like he is currently, we could add another five to seven employees through him.

As I think about this now, I realize that the only person at the company I can see as my "successor" is David. As I've written before, I enjoy working with him, customers love him, and he has a lot of creative ideas. Right now I don't think he would feel comfortable running the whole company, but there's nobody else I know that I'd rather turn the company over to.

Getting back to the meeting, I like Rob, and I'm willing to take this chance. Jack is about as okay with it as he's going to be, and while Marty says it's a little unusual, if we're all okay with it, he says it's fine with him.

As we all drive off in our different ways after the meeting, Jack called and reminded me not to give away anything important when I meet with Rob's prospect, that I should just play the role of the technical guy at the meeting, and try not to talk as much as I normally do. A little while after that Marty called to ask me what I thought, and I told him I like Rob. He told me Rob said the same thing about us, and he was pretty excited. I asked him about Rob's financial sources, and while he didn't give me any names, he said Rob's family has connections with influential people in town, and if they thought this was a good idea and they trusted Rob, they should be able to come up with at least $2M.

It's been just over two weeks since our breakfast meeting, and Rob and I met his prospect late this afternoon at the prospect's office.

The first thing to say is that Rob drives a sweet car, a red sports car of some sort. He told me he owns it outright, and I'm thinking that if that's the truth, he can sell it and at least have a $40K down payment to buy the company.

The funny thing is, I've owned this company all these years, and I still drive the same car I fondly refer to as "the crapmobile" I had when I started the company. When I was Rob's age I had several nice cars, all brand new, but as I've gotten older I don't care about cars too much, as long as they're comfortable and reliable.

As Rob and I walked from the parking lot to the main entrance of the building I asked him several questions to try to get as comfortable as I can in this role. Having owned my own business for all these years, I'm surprisingly uncomfortable at going into a meeting and feeling muzzled. He assures me that if the client asks any questions about our relationship he'll handle them, and again, we can fall back to our "partnering" approach if need be.

The meeting with the prospect went very well, and I liked working with Rob. He's everything you'd want in a salesperson: smart, enthusiastic, honest, likable, and the prospect has been well-qualified. Rob also knows what he's talking about technically, and I found myself wondering again if he can be the project manager we're looking for. For two people that barely know each other going into the meeting, everything is as smooth as can be. If our situations were reversed I'd gladly hire him.

As our meeting started to wrap up, I realized that one of us was going to have to write up a proposal for this prospect, and as we approached the point in the meeting where it's time to tell the prospect this is the next step, I'm prepared to say that I'll do it, but Rob says just the right thing, that "we" will have a proposal to him within a few days. The prospect doesn't press us on a date, so Rob and I are spared a discussion of how we'll work this into our schedules.

On the way out to the parking lot Rob and I talk about the proposal, and he tells me that if I can write up the technical part, he'll plug it into his standard format. I told him I can't get it written up tomorrow, but that I should have it for him Saturday afternoon. I ask how he thought it went, and he said it was great, he really enjoyed working with me. I told him I enjoyed it as well, and we drove off in our separate directions. So far, so good.

I wrote up the proposal for Rob's prospect and sent it to him yesterday. I don't have any feedback on it yet, but it was all pretty straightforward, by the book. I wrote the proposal like I normally would, but lowered the overall time estimate slightly compared to what I would normally make it. I didn't want to deceive Rob about our skills in relation to the business sale, but thinking of the advice from Marty (most businesses aren't sold to the first buyer) and Jack (don't give anything away), I thought that if everything fell apart between us and Rob, and we were going to be competitors on future deals, I wanted him to think we were faster than we really were.

I'm surprised Jack hasn't contacted me to see how things went, but David and I had a few emails back and forth, discussing what I should or shouldn't include in my part of the proposal. After our back and forth, we decided that there wasn't any secret sauce in the technical work, that almost anyone who heard what I heard would draw up the same solution.

Really, if there's any secret sauce in meeting with prospects like this, the biggest thing is really listening to what they're saying. You have to have empathy for their situation, ask a lot of questions to find out what they're comfortable with and where they're going, and then decide on the best approach for their particular situation. After that you just sketch up some industry-standard diagrams that show what you're thinking, and add a cost proposal to it.

It feels weird, but this proposal is out of my hands now. I'm curious to see if "we" will get the job, but all I can do now is wait.

I got word today that nothing is going to happen with Marty's other potential buyer. Apparently our asking price was too steep for them to even bother with a meeting. Frankly, this really pisses me off, because it either means Marty was bluffing and didn't have another prospect, he didn't do all of his legwork to qualify this prospect, or his asking price scared them off.

If you're not familiar with the phrase, "qualifying a prospect," in my mind it means (a) making sure they have a real budget for the project we're talking about, and (b) making sure we're talking to the real decision maker. In my experience, a bad salesperson will drag me around to talk to anyone, and a good salesperson will make sure I'm talking to a qualified prospect.

I mentioned earlier that Rob did a good job of qualifying the prospect that we met with, and since my early days of consulting, this has always been a flash point for me. When you think about it, a sales meeting is going to cost an employer hundreds of dollars in labor costs, maybe thousands, and when you're in the business of selling a limited resource like *time*, in a sales meeting you're allocating that limited resource to a non-billing activity. If the salesperson hasn't qualified the prospect, you can really throw money away fast.

Any time we hire a salesperson I tell them up front, "I don't want to take our technical people out of a paid gig to go to a sales meeting with an unqualified prospect," and unless there's a big potential pot of gold at stake, it drives me insane to go on a sales call where a client hasn't been qualified. (Okay, okay, we did generate several hundred thousand dollars in revenue from one client that was completely unqualified, but we had been trying to get in to see them for years, so when they finally called us one day, we jumped. This is the only successful exception to the qualified prospect rule I can recall.)

Assuming these potential buyers really exist, it feels like Marty didn't qualify them at all. I mean, he told us he thought he thought he had a potential buyer, told us our company was worth over $5M, we told him we're willing to sell for $2M, but now the prospect thinks our price is too steep? This doesn't add up, and I'm pissed. I just had a long workout before writing this to try to burn off some energy, but I'm still furious.

THURSDAY, DECEMBER 12, 2002

I've had a few more phone calls with Marty and Rob over the last few days, mostly just clarifying the financial information we've already sent. Rob also tried to get a little more information about our clients, but I refused to give out any specific names, or what sort of work we were doing for any particular client. As far as I was concerned, they had the blinded customer information, which showed things like "X yearly revenue coming from Customer Y," and in my mind that's all they needed right now. I assured them that if we went further in our conversations the numbers and the customer names would match up.

There was no word yet on whether Rob had gotten the project with the prospect we met with, but it was still early, so I didn't expect much. Rob was happy with what I wrote up, and that's really all I wanted to know.

Late last night there was a flurry of emails, and in short, today Jack and I met again with Rob and Marty, but this time we also met two of Rob's potential financial backers.

We met at the office of a well-known, local CPA firm. The CPA we met with is Rob's accountant, and a managing partner of this firm. Another local businessman named Jim was there, and although I've heard his name before, I've never met him.

Neither of these men work directly in the computer field, though the CPA told us he has several clients who are small computer consulting firms, and he's familiar with their financials. As you can imagine, there was a little small talk at the beginning, and after we all got to know each other's backgrounds a little more, we dove into the numbers, with Jim and the CPA asking all the questions.

It occurred to me that we suddenly went from Rob -- an energetic yet inexperienced young man -- to two men who are probably in their fifties, very experienced, and their questions were very thorough. They pushed as far as they could on every financial number, and I gave them what I felt comfortable with. In a few cases I asked why they needed to know something, or told them I'm not comfortable giving them additional details at this point, and they backed off easily.

To be clear, I did try to answer as many of their questions as thoroughly as possible, because I know they're trying to make an honest decision about whether or not to buy our company. But when they also asked the names of specific customers, or who is working on what project, that was pressing a bit too far for me. I feel like I've said this a million times by now, but I reassured them that if there's a firm offer on the table, I'll be glad to match customer names up to the revenue numbers, but I hope they can understand I didn't feel comfortable doing that today.

To his credit, Marty told us before the meeting what to expect, and to only answer questions we felt comfortable with, and that there was no offer on the table at this time. He said the men were aware that we were looking to sell for around $3M (Marty's number, not ours), and they were financial men trying to understand their potential investment. Marty told us that if everything went forward, eventually there would be a "Letter of Intent" to buy the company, and at that point we should be ready to share everything.

I was impressed that their questions were very thorough, but not insulting in any way. They're clearly business people interested in the bottom line, and they're thorough in their work, which I respect, but they're also nice in their approach. Assuming these are men I'll have to work with in the future, I'm sizing them up as much as they're sizing me up. It may sound weird, but I also want to make a good impression with them, so in case this deal falls through, they'll consider working with us in the future, assuming they even need custom software written, or a website designed.

The meeting ended cordially, and I feel like I've given them all the information I'm comfortable sharing at this time. I don't feel like my refusal to give away more details has hurt us. Actually, in one case, since my name was recently in the local business paper in regards to one of our customers, I told them yes, that customer was one of our top five customers, and as far as I knew they would be customers for life, and they could certainly talk to our contacts there when the time was right.

After the meeting, Marty told us that we're now in a "wait and see" process to see what these men will want to do next.

In other news, we landed a nice new account just prior to this meeting, so our business continues to roll along. I can't stress enough how important it is to keep your regular business running on all cylinders as you go through this process.

MONDAY, DECEMBER 16, 2002

Marty called me late this afternoon to tell me that Rob and the gentlemen we met with Friday would like to present an offer to us. At first I was pretty excited, and amazed at their turnaround time, but Marty also told me that he doesn't know anything about the offer, that the men want to present it to all of us at the same time. I'm taking this as a bad sign, because if they have to meet with us to present their offer it's probably going to be a sales pitch of some sort. Think about it this way: Whenever you've sold a house, did a potential buyer ever request a meeting to present their offer, or did their realtor just tell your realtor what their offer was? I would have expected them to at least ask Marty if he thought we would take "X" for the company, just to test the water.

On the good news front, this time of year is usually open for meetings, as we spend a lot of time going to holiday parties and delivering gifts to our clients, so setting up a meeting time is pretty simple. We'll meet this Wednesday, again at the CPA's office.

I've relayed this information to Jack and David, and as usual, Jack will be coming to the meeting with me while David won't. (At this point, even if David wanted to come to the meeting I'd have to say no to him, as I don't want to introduce anyone new into the process right now.) They both share the same concern that I do, that not getting a written offer before a meeting is probably a bad sign.

In other news, if I didn't mention it before, all the partners are now using personal email addresses for our communications. After a recent email gaffe at the company, we decided it would be better not to use our email system for these conversations any more.

WEDNESDAY, DECEMBER 18, 2002

Late this afternoon we met with the same group of people at the CPA's office to listen to their offer to buy our company. In short, the two financial men told us they'd be willing to offer a total of $1.4M, with most of that paid out from the company's earnings over a period of thirty-six months. Jack and I would have to stay at the company that entire time, and they made it very clear this is as high as they can go, this isn't a negotiation.

At the meeting Rob smiles, but is forced to sit in the background, and barely says a word; things are clearly out of his hands now. The owner of the CPA firm gives most of the presentation, with Marty, Jack, and I asking questions as we go along.

A few things stand out for me:

- We'd have to guarantee that we'd stay at the company for the entire three years. This seems like a very long time to stay with people that I don't even know if I'll like. I can take a beating from someone for a while, maybe a year, but three years, guaranteed?

- Our salaries would be $80K per year, so the total compensation during this time would be that salary and our shares of the $1.4M.

- Calculating the numbers in my head, this didn't seem like much of a "deal" to me. If I just worked at the company for three more years and then just handed the keys to someone and walked away, I'd be making nearly as much money.

Frankly, I'm upset and confused, though I'm trying not to show the upset part. Really, I'm more confused than upset. Maybe this is a good offer, and there's something I don't understand?

At the end of the meeting Jack and I thanked them for their time and consideration, and we told them we'll think about this, but that it's significantly lower than what we had in mind. I shook Rob's hand with the feeling that I won't be seeing him again, which is a big disappointment.

After the meeting Jack, Marty, and I talked in the parking lot for a while. I asked Marty several times if there was something I was missing, if their offer was somehow better than us just walking away in three years without selling, and he said no, that seemed about right to him. He said accountants are notoriously conservative, and he felt this was a lowball offer. He also said he was disappointed they wouldn't share it with him over the phone, because he could have saved everyone a lot of time. He added that having to stay for the full thirty-six months was also unusual, that very few owners stay on more than 12-18 months after a sale.

Jack and I quickly agreed we wouldn't accept this offer, and told Marty that if they wanted to increase their offer to our minimum amount or higher, without having to be paid out over 36 months, we'd be glad to meet with them again, but seeing that they made it clear this was their best offer, we all assumed we'd be moving on.

While it's nice to hear an offer to buy our company this fast, this was also a big disappointment.

I called David on the way home and told him the news. He agreed that we shouldn't accept the offer, and he thought it was strange that they would even bother making it. I also told my wife about it when I got home, and with no other prospects on the table, I assume that business life is going to go back to normal for a while.

The only positive things I can find in this experience are that we've been down this road now and heard one offer, and it gave us a chance to meet Rob, and maybe our paths will cross again one day.

With Christmas coming in the middle of this week, and the New Year's holiday coming in the middle of next week, work will be light for most of our consultants. But for me and my team, we'll be going live with a large, new project just after New Year's Day, so work will be as hard as it gets.

Earlier this summer there was a problem with this client when I had to go out of town on another consulting gig, and George took my place. As with any conflict, I don't know exactly what happened, but the relationship with the client was strained for quite some time, and only lately, as we get closer to delivering the first phase of this project, do things feel normal again.

Or at least I thought they did. The client brought this incident up again Friday, though I don't know why, even after I asked why we were talking about this again. I assume it's because they're nervous about the project launch going smoothly.

Nothing else has happened on the business sales front. Marty said he talked to Rob's investors one more time last week, but they weren't budging at all, and he thought that deal was dead. I told Marty I was interested in hiring Rob, but he suggested I wait a little while. He said Rob was still very motivated to buy the company, and he might be successful in persuading other people to finance him.

We came very close to making George and Cooper Class A partners recently, but after some problems George had with a second client recently, we decided to hold off on the promotion. We could make Cooper a Class A Partner without promoting George at the same time, but they've been friends for a long time, and we didn't want to make the situation with George any worse than it already is, so we're holding off on both for the time being. Jack said that George's ego is a little wounded right now, and he doesn't need another blow to his confidence.

It's a month since my last entry, and the conflict that occurred between George and my client last summer just ended up costing us some money in the form of a pretty big refund/discount to our client. When I say big, I mean "five-figure big," which is very large, considering I've never given a refund to a customer before.

What probably helped drive this is that we're a little late going live on our project, but what concerned the customer more than being late was being over budget, and as we kept talking about being over budget, they kept bringing up the problems from last summer, when they said a lot of money was wasted. I've come to like and respect these people, and beyond that, I'd also like to keep their business, so offering a refund/discount seems like the right thing to do on several fronts.

After several meetings and my own research into the situation, the client and I agreed to a "refund" amount. As I was talking to my client I kept bouncing my thoughts off of Jack and David. They again suggested that I not say anything to George because of his other recent client problems.

That's a little hard for me, because I've always told anyone I've hired that they'll never have a bad yearly review with me. When they ask why that is, I tell them it's because if I ever have a problem with them, they'll hear it from me right away, I don't wait for reviews. But now Jack and (to some extent) David are telling me to go away from my instincts here, and I'm trying to respect and understand that.

What's rumbling through my mind tonight is if/when it's ever going to be a good idea to make George a Class A Partner. If I didn't mention it before, the reason for this concern is that it's harder to get rid of a Class A partner if I ever need to. With a Class B partner, I can just pay them book value for their shares, and take their ownership back away from them, but with a Class A partner that process is much more involved, and could involve business valuations and lawyers.

This is actually the third problem we've had between George and our clients -- I skipped the first incident, which happened a few years ago -- and with Jack and David telling me not to discuss these problems with George, at least not strongly and directly, I'm not willing to make him a Class A partner, not until this problem is addressed.

I also have to wonder what would have happened if we were in the process of selling the business to Rob and his financial backers and this came up. No doubt it would have complicated the sale.

Four months have passed since we signed the agreement with Marty, and very little has happened with him. I've talked to him a few times when he said he had some queries, but we haven't met with anyone else, at least not until today. Marty asked if we wanted to talk to some potential buyers who were a real long shot, and with nothing else going on, I said sure, why not. That led to this morning's meeting, which goes down as one of the strangest business encounters I can recall.

Although he couldn't be there due to a previous commitment, Marty set up a breakfast meeting for Jack and I with a couple from a nearby state who have roots in this area. They're considering moving back to Kentucky, and the husband has indirectly worked with software developers in his current work, while his wife has some design and marketing experience. I don't know this for fact, but my impression was that they have a lot of money, and they're trying to figure out what to do next in their lives.

What this really reminded me of was meeting the couple from the 1970s television series *Hart to Hart*, where a rich couple (Stephanie Powers and Robert Wagner) went around solving crimes (for some reason I can't remember). Except in our case the rich couple was thinking about buying our business instead of solving crimes. At one point, when I realized the meeting wasn't going anywhere, I took a bio-break, and looked around the restaurant to see if their butler "Max" was in the restaurant, or parked outside.

Suffice it to say, nothing is going to happen here. Marty told me this was a long shot, and he was right. This encounter makes me wonder how many people like this Marty talks to that we never hear from? That's certainly one benefit of having a business broker trying to sell your business.

A month has passed since the meeting with the "Hart to Hart" couple. As expected, nothing further happened with them.

To help with his efforts, Marty asked us to think about our competition a little more, and put together a list of companies that we thought we be interested in buying us, both regionally and nationally. I put together a few names of companies in our area that do what we do, and are generally larger than we are, but I don't know anyone at those businesses. I also added in the names of a couple of companies that don't do what we do, but who might be interested in the "synergy" of adding our skill set to theirs. He again promised not to give out our company name, and will only send out the usual blinded information.

I talked about this with Jack and David, and we debated about giving Marty the name of our closest competitor. I should take that back; we gave him that name a long time ago, but we told him to avoid them. If they found out our business was for sale they could use that against us in sales meetings, which could be disastrous. But with nothing else happening, Jack, David, and I talked about this once more, though we again decided against it.

One observation I'll add here is that I think it would be helpful if Marty knew more about our business and specialized in our industry. Just like Jack and I have built up contacts in our industry that makes our sales job easier, I'm sure this would be easier if Marty had people he could call that he already knew. I assume his current approach is some form of advertising and possibly cold-calling, and that's a much harder approach.

In other news, our business keeps chugging along. There's no business growth, but we're not getting smaller either.

A local company that we've partnered with in the past was just sold. This doesn't affect our business in any way, but I decided to use the event as an excuse to write a business acquaintance named Jerry who owns another small business here in town. I've met him at several local business events, and I've come to like him quite a bit.

Technically you could argue that our companies are competitors, but we worked together on a project recently, with them taking care of one part of the project and us doing something else. The project went well, and I enjoyed working with his team. They also tend to focus on a few specific vertical markets, such as integrating accounting systems, where we provide more horizontal solutions (general computer programming and web design), so I don't think of them as competitors as much as potential collaborators.

From a personnel perspective I know they have two good salespeople who I'd hire, and at least one technical person who can run a project. So in my email to Jerry, I mentioned it was a pleasure working on that recent project together, and I also mentioned the sale of this other company. I wrote that if he was ever interested in a merger of some sort, I'd be glad to discuss that with him.

He wrote back and said he wasn't interested in a merger at this time, but would certainly welcome a lunch together, and we quickly set up a lunch date.

I told Jack about this, and to my surprise, he seemed to take real offense at my contacting Jerry. The nicest way to describe his response when I told him I was going to lunch with Jerry was that it was "curt." I don't know where that came from. Maybe he's upset about something else, or he doesn't like Jerry, or their company, or maybe he's upset that I've taken this into my own hands. I really don't know, I can only speculate, because when I asked Jack what he was upset about, he denied being upset, but I had the impression the hair was standing up on his back.

The lunch meeting with Jerry went well. I began by reiterating what I mentioned in the email, that if he was ever interested in a merger of some sort, I was very open, that I anted to grow the company. After that brief discussion I dropped the matter, and we focused on how we could work better together. We talked about areas where we might compete (very few), and where we could work together without competing.

To be clear, I didn't mention that our business was for sale, and in fact, the idea of adding Jerry and his people to our company is something that would reenergize me, and I'd drop the idea of selling our company. (No telling what I'd have to say to Marty if/when that time comes.)

I stopped off at the office and shared the conversation details with Jack, but he still seemed very short with me. My current guess is that Jack sees Jerry as a competitor to his job. If so, that's not a healthy attitude for someone to have, assuming we're trying to grow the business. As I've mentioned, running a fifteen-person business has become routine/boring to me, and if you're thinking about growing a larger, healthy company, you want to hire strong people, potential leaders of that company. If Jack looks at it that way, he may have a smaller piece of the pie if we bought out Jerry's company, but it would be a much larger pie.

Oh well, so much for whatever improvements Jack and I have had in our relationship recently.

As I had lunch with Jerry, I remained very impressed with him, and I can see why customers do business with him; he's smart, friendly, and likable. Shoot, give me Jerry and Rob and we'd sell a ton of business, though I still don't know enough good technical people to fulfill it. I'm now more convinced than ever that finding good technical talent is our biggest problem, and we need to find a way to break through that hurdle.

I keep running the idea of hiring a dedicated Project Manager past the partners and our clients, but the partners don't like the idea, and this isn't a role our clients want to pay for. But with our inability to find a strong technical person who can also run projects, I think it's something we have to do. In the same way that our web design team is a "loss leader," this person can also be a loss leader, one that will help us hire additional programmers.

Ugh ... Jack and David had lunch with two non-partner employees today, and as they were talking about the other company that was recently sold, when one of the employees said something about the sale (I don't know what), Jack replied, "Every company is for sale at the right price." While that may be true, that's not something that's going to give an employee a great feeling at any time, and I certainly didn't think it was something to say right now.

David and I were working together this afternoon, and when we were alone for a few moments he told me about this, and I just cringed.

I've been away from the office for a while and was generally unreachable (in a lot of meetings), so Marty called Jack to tell him that he had another prospect he wanted us to meet, a company here in town, and he was sending them our blinded information. I don't know if this is our major competitor, or someone else, but a vague message like that sure leaves a guy wondering.

Thursday, July 10, 2003

We have the information on the prospect Marty told us about, and they are a local competitor, though they tend to work in a different area of the city than we do, so we don't run into them much. (Most people don't know it, but Louisville, Kentucky is the sixteenth-largest city in the United States, so although it isn't a huge city, it definitely has different "areas.") I've heard their name, but to my knowledge we've never competed directly against each other. I also know their lawyer, a person I talked to when I was first looking for a business attorney. He's worked up a questionnaire for us to respond to, and to put it mildly, it's very detailed.

The questionnaire they sent us was twenty pages long, and including the following sections, with specific questions in each section they wanted us to respond to:

- Corporate records
- Employee matters
- Government regulations and filings
- Intellectual properties
- Liens and security interests
- Litigation, disputes, and claims
- Loan agreement and other financial arrangements
- Marketing
- Material agreements
- Miscellaneous
- Real estate
- Research and development
- Security measures
- Warranties

In many ways our business is very simple, and because (a) this company is a local competitor and (b) the paperwork seemed like a boilerplate document that was more appropriate for a huge corporation than a small LLC, we often answered just Yes, No, or N/A to many of the questions. We also decided to skip many other questions, writing "Available after a Letter of Intent."

Although we now know the name of this company, we haven't met with them yet, so a lot of these questions are premature. If it seems that I'm overly cautious about sharing information about our company or clients in preparing these documents, let me share a short story.

A little while ago I got a business deal because one of my competitors had a big mouth, and they were talking publicly about a prospect. They either didn't know I was a competitor, or didn't care, but either way, they babbled on about their customer, including their contact names, at a social engagement. In short, I remembered the names, made a call on this customer, and took their business away. So I hope you can understand that when it comes to strangers asking anything about my business, I don't want to give anything away until we are extremely close to a deal.

This is also where your business broker can act as a sounding board. Marty did say some things, like, "Think about it. Imagine you're the buyer at this stage. Wouldn't you like to know this information?" As a seller you're free to disagree with your broker, and we've certainly done that several times so far, but at least he can be helpful in trying to put you in the shoes of the potential business buyer.

One final note here today: Because I've been working at a client site on another project, Jack and my wife have had to handle most of the paperwork related to this potential buyer, and because I'm working closely with several of our employees at this client site, I've had to be very careful about taking Jack's phone calls. After his first call I put the phone on vibrate, and while he probably called me five times, I only answered the first two times, finally calling him back later in the day when I was alone. I'm very concerned about my employees seeing any changes in my behavior, and it's hard to answer Jack's questions when I'm sharing a room with several of our employees.

After taking the time to answer all the questions from this prospect, discussing amongst ourselves what we wanted to share and not share, and me dealing with all the phone calls from Jack, nothing at all came from this other company, and I do mean nothing. There wasn't even a follow-up meeting, which really surprised me.

Marty said he called them many times to follow up with them, and couldn't even get through to their owners until today, when they simply told him they "weren't interested." He said he tried to press them for any sort of feedback at all, but they wouldn't say anything else.

All I can say to that is that I'm glad we limited the information we gave them. Well, that, and I won't have much to say to them if I ever run into them at a local social event. What a waste of time.

You can argue that we might have taken another step with this company if we had shared more information, but I think they were just on a fishing expedition, to learn what they could about our company. They spent a few hundred dollars on attorney's fees to get whatever they could from us, and I'm very glad we limited our answers.

I do feel vulnerable now that a potential competitor knows that our business is for sale, and that upsets me as much as anything. According to all the legal papers they had to sign, they can't say that they know our business is for sale to anyone, but if they're real scumbags I'm sure they could imply something like that. I'm not happy with this at all, and I just hope it doesn't come back to bite us.

I've been traveling a lot lately, both in town and out of town, and I'm beat. Our business continues to chug along at the same pace, and there haven't been any inquiries from Marty lately. That's pretty disappointing, as we're coming up to our one-year anniversary of first hearing from Marty, but I've been so busy with work that I really don't think about it too much.

To give you an idea of how weird it is to have your company for sale, much of what I've been doing lately is giving public speeches within our industry about certain techniques and processes I've learned. That has resulted in some interviews with the local press, and in one instance my photo again ended up on the front page of the local business newspaper. So *publicly*, I may look like some sort of industry leader, while *privately* my company is for sale. I don't mind this; if anything, it should help make our company more valuable. But it's an unusual feeling.

Wednesday, November 12, 2003

I didn't mention it in my last note, but to get any of that information about my speeches on our website, I had to write the press releases myself. In a small company I tend to associate 'sales' and 'marketing' together, so I assumed this was something Jack would handle, but I finally just wrote the releases myself to get them out there. From a business perspective, what's the use of doing all these speeches if you're not going to use them in your own PR?

While our PR sucks, I was able to use my series of speeches in a sales meeting today. When a customer said that one of his employees was going to a particular trade show, I casually mentioned that I had spoken their recently, and it was a wonderful conference. I won't say we got the deal because of this, but the meeting did go from (a) us trying to sell ourselves to them to (b) a long conversation where all I had to do was answer their questions. People can say whatever they want about PR, but this was a sweet six-figure deal, made much easier because I had given these talks and worked with the press.

FRIDAY, NOVEMBER 14, 2003

Bummer. A little more than a year has come and gone now since we first spoke to Marty, and I haven't heard anything from him recently, other than some polite "just checking in" phone calls from him. I find myself thinking about that first potential deal with Rob, but then I remember that wasn't much of a deal at all.

Friday, April 16, 2004

Thanksgiving, Christmas, New Year's Day, and a new spring have all come and gone since my last entry here. Yesterday was tax day, and after more than a year and a half with Marty, we have no prospects to buy our business. Some days I feel just fine with that, and other days I daydream about selling the business and going off on a nice, long vacation.

Our business is still doing fine, but we're also still more or less stuck at fifteen employees. I won't belabor this point, as I've already written about it enough. I have started an in-house training project, trying to train the people we have to run projects, so we can then hire new employees to backfill their positions, but as I'm sure you can imagine, not all geeks are cut out to run projects. This is also hard to do at a small consulting firm, because we're paid by the billable hour, so we need to strike a balance between training these guys and also getting our billable time in.

As usual, the emotionally taxing part of this for me is that I want to either grow the company, buy someone else's business (like Jerry's), or sell our business to someone who can help me grow it. But every time I try to talk to my partners about this, Jack doesn't seem to have any interest in it at all; David supports me, but can't help here; George seems indifferent, like "If it happens, it happens"; and Cooper seems very interested in the prospect, but like David is primarily a technical person who can't help here.

In general we don't talk about selling the business too much. I usually just report at our partner meetings that there isn't any new news, and try to encourage everyone to keep thinking about taking care of our current clients, and to think about how we can grow the company.

Sunday, June 6, 2004

After twenty years of marriage, my wife and I have separated.

I've avoided mentioning anything about this here until now because I didn't think it was relevant to the process of selling the business, but now that we're separated, it's important to mention it.

I've been staying at an extended stay hotel for a few weeks, and just moved into an apartment. I told Jack and David about this shortly after the separation, so they would understand if my wife and I seemed to act any differently. But I also told them that I wanted everything to be "business as usual" for everyone at work. That may sound difficult, but I'm out of the office 90% of the time now, so it's not like we see each other all the time.

Also, our separation is as amicable as a separation can be, and in many ways we get along better now that we're separated. (Shoot, I get along better with her now than I have with Jack for the last few years.) I don't want to get into the details too much, but I will say that I've found it very hard to be married to someone I work with. At night our conversations usually deteriorated into shop talk, and that's not really something I want in a marriage.

Yesterday I told our junior partners what was going on, and today I shared the news with the four employees I work with most of the time. That leaves a couple of employees at the office who won't learn about this directly from me, but my wife is going to tell them about this, as she's good friends with them, and I don't see them much anyway.

In unrelated news, a few more things have come up recently with Jack, and in short, I'm contemplating making an offer to buy his ownership shares back from him. Actually, I'm being polite here. What I'm really doing tonight is reviewing our business Operating Agreement to see what my options with him are, and buying his shares back seems like the easiest way out of our problems.

There's a difficult situation here, though. Jack's wife plays an important role at the company, and even he has said that she's more important to the company than he is. I don't know if he's having a crisis of confidence (like he said George was having), or if he's still unhappy about his role at the company, but as I try to look at this without any emotion, I think the best thing to do is to buy him out of the company, let him leave, and make his wife a partner. Of course that's much easier said than done.

Marty told me that our closest competitor has been inquiring about this "mystery" computer business for sale. I don't know if he contacted them, or they contacted him, but since this has come up, Marty tells me we have to do something about it. He assures me he hasn't given them our name yet, and says that our options are (a) to give them the usual "blinded" information as Step 1 in the process, or (b) let him tell them that the mystery business isn't for sale to them. Since there are no other prospects, his advice is to meet with them.

Marty assures us that once they sign an NDA (nondisclosure agreement) as part of the process, they can't legally say anything to anyone, and we can sue them if they ever use the information that our company is for sale in any way. That's huge, because we still run into them fairly often, and I can see them saying "Oh, it's just a rumor, but I heard they were for sale," when they talk to a prospect about us. But hey, they could say the same thing today, telling their prospects there is this mystery computer consulting business for sale in the local area, and of course the description sure does match our business.

I'm very torn about this idea. I *don't like it* more than I *like it*, but I also want to sell the company or grow it. I've met with owners of this other business several times at business functions, and while there's one of them I don't care for, the others seem okay, and they're certainly aggressive.

I met with David and Jack yesterday to discuss this, and we weighed the pros and cons. In the end we decided we were pretty screwed either way, and it might be better to get them under an NDA, so we decided to go forward with it. I called Marty today, and he's going to get them to sign his NDA before going any further, and we'll see what happens. I also warned him that if he thought I haven't given away much information previously, this was going to be even worse for him.

Marty, Jack, and I had breakfast with the three owners of our closest competitor today. I tend to be very competitive myself, and at least from my standpoint this meeting began very uncomfortably. Greeting your competitor, then looking at them across the table, with the thought of them buying your company, isn't very pleasant, and frankly, it made me want to puke. But I agreed to this meeting, and told myself to suck it up.

Both sides opened up as the meeting went on, and we even laughed about a few of our competitions against each other. They asked what I did on one of the six-figure deals we stole from them, and I told them I'd be glad to share that information after the sale.

One of our competitions

The story of stealing this deal from them is one of my favorite stories in the history of our company. Although I was at home with the flu -- the real flu, not a cold -- Jack called and told me we were going to lose this $300K+ deal, and I had to go to lunch with the president of our prospect's company to see if I could salvage it.

Heavily medicated, I met with the customer, and listened to her concerns (while having to take two bathroom breaks to cough and blow my nose, to put it politely). She wasn't very happy with our company at all to that point, so I agreed with Jack's assessment that we were going to lose the deal.

And then at one point during the lunch when I thought her attitude towards us had improved a little, it occurred to me that while she was thinking one thing about her project, the project was really about something quite different, something we were much better at than our competitor. So I said, "I don't know much about your project, I've left that to our team members to work out. But if your project is mostly about web design, then you'll be fine going with either our company or our competitor, but if your project is mostly about computer programming, our company is in much better shape there. We have full-time programmers we've hired from companies like IBM, while our competitor outsources work like that."

I didn't say anything else, and just let her talk about what she thought her project was really about. As she spoke, I think it occurred to her that the project was indeed mostly about computer programming. (I'd later learn that 80% of the budget was for programming, and 20% was for web design.)

While she didn't sign the contract there at the table -- we didn't even bring one -- she called Jack later in the afternoon to tell us we had won the deal.

Getting back to our meeting with our competitors this morning, they laughed uncomfortably about that deal. I don't know much about their financials, but I know that one deal was almost 1/6th of our revenue for the entire year, and it would have hurt us if we didn't get it.

About our competitor

After the uncomfortable beginning, our meeting became very interesting, and I can see why customers would do business with these guys. They approach business very differently than we do, and I'm sure they leave customers with a very different impression than we do, but they seem very aggressive, competent, and likable. They did a lot of investigative work on us, and knew most of our customers, all the speaking engagements I had done, etc.

Why do you want to sell your business?

The most interesting question we run into at all of these meetings, including that first meeting with Marty, is "Why do you want to sell your business?" As a seller, you really have to be prepared to answer this question, because as I've learned, potential buyers ask it over and over again in different ways. I won't say they think you're lying, but I do think they're trying very hard to learn what problems there might be, why you *really* want to sell.

By now my usual response is that I could do this job for the rest of my life if we could just solve a couple of problems, primarily getting my schedule down to less than sixty hours a week, and finding good people to run projects. This isn't a lie, I really think I could do this for quite a while longer, especially if we got the hours under control. It's one thing to work all hours of the week when you're in your twenties and thirties, and something completely different to keep doing this in your forties. Other than the extra long work hours (without being able to grow the company), I generally like what I'm doing.

Getting back to our breakfast, things ended up well enough. Besides talking about business competitions and customers, we talked about most of our financials, and did the usual thing with their questions, answering the ones we were comfortable with, and putting of the others until things got more serious.

I hope they got the information they needed, while also understanding our reluctance to share too much information. In the end it was also nice to see them as more human. Given my sports background, I won't go crazy and admit that I like them, but I can respect them as competitors. Their understanding of business finances is solid, and their research on us was impressive.

MONDAY, JULY 26, 2004

Almost two weeks have passed since my last entry. For a few days there was a flurry of information exchanged with our competitors through Marty, generally trying to clear up some financial information. As usual they asked more questions and we replied "After the Letter of Intent." With all of this activity they certainly seemed like they were doing their due diligence.

But then today they called Marty and told them they weren't going to go any farther down this road, and there wasn't going to be any sort of offer ... nothing, zilch, nada. I want to call their primary owner personally to see what has happened, but Marty has been trying to convince me that isn't a good idea. I don't see why it isn't a good idea, but I told him I wouldn't do it, at least not today.

At this point the idea of running *everything* through a business broker is beginning to annoy me. I give him kudos, he got us talking with these guys, and I like them more than I want to admit. But now I think he just needs to get out of the way and let me help close the deal.

I did something like this to a realtor when I bought a house about ten years ago. The deal had fallen through, and my realtor told me the people selling the house were taking the house off the market and going to Florida for the winter in a few days. So I did an end run around the realtor, handed a letter to the owners of the home, basically telling them we'd expedite the deal in every way, and if they went to Florida just a little bit later, their house would be sold, and they wouldn't have to worry about it any more. Suffice it to say, they sold the house to us.

So when I say that I want Marty to get out of the way, that's what I mean. I have a huge interest in this, I can help close the deal, step aside.

I also had a very long talk with Marty today about what price he's been giving customers. He said he's been leaving it as open as he can, not suggesting a buying price to potential buyers, but I have to wonder if he isn't saying $3M or $5M at some point. Again, way back when, I did my own business valuation on our company, and I could rationalize somewhere around $1.5M to $2.5M (ballpark), but not $3M. If I'm a buyer, and he's telling me $3M, and I'm thinking "$2M, tops," I don't think I'd bother to make an offer either.

Argh, I don't know if any of this is true, and I'm probably just writing this because I'm upset. This is the second competitor who now knows that our business is for sale, and it's making me feel really vulnerable.

A few weeks have passed since my last entry here, and now I understand why our competitor didn't make an offer to buy our business: They just hired one of our best employees, certainly our best employee who was not a partner.

Some of the people at the office have told me he's been a handful to deal with for months now, and they have mixed emotions about losing him, but I'm not in that group. He is an extremely talented person, possibly one of the best designers in the country. This is a big blow to us, and I suspect our competitors knew that it would be.

This raises all sorts of questions about what just happened, and as you can imagine, some of the partners are pretty pissed off. I am too, but I know what information we gave them, and what they already had, so I know they didn't use the information we gave them to "steal" our employee. His work is extremely well known in local circles, and our clients all rave about his work. But it does smell bad, and I'm pretty pissed, too.

Two things are running through my mind. First, he's going to go over there, and he may learn that our business is for sale. If that happens, will he turn around and tell anyone here? Second, we need to do something fast to replace him, because several of our projects go through him.

Marty's NDA

I called Marty this afternoon to vent a little at him, and talk about the legal issues. He tells me that there's nothing in his NDA to cover an issue like this, and this brings up a very important point that I've never seen the NDA he has prospective buyers sign, and that was a failure on my part. So I asked him to send me a copy.

I wrote about this months ago, but I recently came across an article about business brokers, and one of the assertions of the article was that you need to be careful about the business broker you select, with a key consideration being whether he knows your industry. I like Marty, but I don't think he knows our industry very well, and I have to wonder if another broker would have additional wording in his NDA to cover something like this.

Again, yes, I'm very upset about this, but I really don't think our competitor learned anything from us that helped them steal this employee. I know what information they had before the meeting, and after it. If anything, this was just extremely bad timing, and I'm sure they think this will be a big enough blow to us that we aren't worth as much as we were worth a few weeks ago. At this very moment that's true, but our people at the office tell me they've found some excellent candidates to replace him.

My biggest concern right now is that the competitor tries to skirt around Marty's NDA in some way, so I told Marty I was going to call the competitor to talk to him about this, but Marty suggested that I let him handle it. I told him that was fine, I was probably upset and the conversation might not go well, but that he needed to forcefully remind him about the NDA.

I've reviewed Marty's NDA, and indeed there isn't anything in there that addresses a potential buyer hiring any of our people. I've asked Marty to add something to his agreement before we talk to any other prospective buyers, and he said he'd do what he can, but this situation hadn't come up before. His business brokerage is part of a nationwide firm of business brokers, so he's going to go back to them to see what other NDA forms they might have.

Consulting business non-competition agreements

Like most other professional service firms, we have a non-competition ("noncompete") agreement with our employees, and while many firms have extremely strict noncompete rules, ours is fairly simple, and more open than other companies I know about. I believe this fair approach has helped us keep employees on board, as they don't feel overly threatened by it, though Jack and George would prefer that it was more aggressive.

The last company I worked at before starting this business had a noncompete agreement that almost kept me from working for one year. Their agreement started as one thing, and then as their business grew, they kept adding more clauses to cover other geographic regions, and before I knew it, it was almost impossible for me to work for another computer company. I almost took a job with Novell just to get out of that agreement, but I changed my mind, and eventually took another job as a computer specialist for a business that was never a customer of the consulting company where I had been working.

As a result of that experience, I decided I would never put someone else through that same experience, so I came up with terms for our noncompete agreement that seemed more fair to me, and if that meant someone could go to work for one of our competitors, well, so be it. If there's a competing company that offers a better work environment than our company, then we've failed anyway, and I don't want a legal agreement to replace us doing the right thing, which is to have the best damn work environment in our industry.

Our web design team found several candidates to replace the designer we lost to our competitor, and I've sat in on final interviews with each one. This is a key position, and I want to see what we're looking at.

An interview with one designer today was weird enough that I thought I'd note it here. For some reason, even though he knew he was meeting new people today, he didn't bother to bring his design portfolio into the meeting. So when I asked if I could see his work, he sighed, like I was putting him out, then said it was in his car, and he would get it.

When he walked out to the car to get his portfolio, I didn't even have to express my opinion, the other people in the room said it themselves, "He's not getting the job."

We finally hired a new designer, and everyone assures me that we'll be just fine. He has a great track record and great references, and he brings a new energy to the team. As I've mentioned before, despite some efforts to make the company a little more interesting, our company does have a "stale" feeling to it, and new blood can be good.

While this brings a close to this situation with our competitor, we're basically back to having no prospects to buy our business. Again I have to wonder, will this competitor use the information that our business is for sale in any way? Will they tell our employee that just went to work for them? In theory those things are illegal, but there are a lot of ways to say things without saying them directly, and I'm again regretting talking to a local competitor about selling our business to them.

I'm very torn on this situation. Part of me never wants to talk to another local competitor again, we've tried it several times now, and we're just giving information away. But the other part thinks we were pretty darn close with these last guys.

David and I did a review with Cooper today, and as reviews go, it was very simple. He's been working with David a lot lately, which is one reason David was there, and I'm told that his work is excellent. He's not an outgoing person at all, but customers love his speed and technical skills, and I've never heard anyone say a bad thing about him.

So the review was very simple, mostly just things like "Keep up the great work," "I appreciate your comments at our partner meetings," and a few similar statements. Before going on, I need to add here that while he has absolutely no interest in sales, he has a real interest in business and marketing, and often sends me ideas by email, which I appreciate, and I try to follow up on all of them.

At lunch today he mentioned that he'd like to be able to buy some more interest in the LLC, even though he knew it was for sale. He said that the company had been for sale for a while, and we hadn't had any luck in selling it, and it might take a while longer to sell, so in the meantime he would like to own a larger portion of it. I told him this caught my by surprise, but I was glad to hear it, and asked him to give me a little while to think about it.

David was fine with Cooper owning more shares, so I tried to talk to Jack about it this afternoon. After waiting to talk to him because he was on the phone with his financial planner, I was surprised to hear Jack say that he thought selling any additional shares to Cooper was a bad idea. He thought Cooper had his opportunities to buy more of the company earlier, and that he now "owns what he owns," and the percentage seemed right to him.

What Jack doesn't know is that I'm more and more convinced that *his* ownership level in the company is too high, and I'm thinking about making another offer to buy back his shares.

In a totally unrelated note, as something of a public service announcement for people who are thinking about separating from their spouse, it's important to mention that all those little errands you used to share with your partner suddenly require much more of your personal time. When you see the owner of a successful small business shopping for groceries at 8 or 9 p.m., it's a safe guess that they're either single, or separated.

Time has flown by, and we're coming up to the end of our two-year sales agreement with Marty. In retrospect I can see why he wanted two years. There aren't many prospects to buy a business, and so far they've all fallen through.

Marty says he has two more potential business buyers, so he's requested a short extension to his listing agreement. I've discussed it briefly in an email stream with my partners, but I've been too busy with a current project to give it much thought yet. I told Marty I wouldn't be able to get back to him with an answer for a few days.

SATURDAY, OCTOBER 23, 2004

While Jack is away on vacation, I met with David, George, and Cooper at the office this morning (Saturday morning), and we decided to give Marty another ninety days to work on his two prospects. We don't know their names, so for all I know he's bluffing, but he still seems like an honest person, and despite all my complaints, I don't mind giving him a little longer. Besides, we've been so busy, I haven't given any thought to working with another business broker.

In hopeful news, I was able to recruit someone we've had our eyes on for a long time. He's reluctant to be a consultant, but I was able to bring him on as a contractor, with the hope that he'll see what we do, and then be willing to come on board full time.

FRIDAY, NOVEMBER 12, 2004

Sometimes things work out so badly all you can do is laugh. In the short time between my last diary entry and this one, a small project our new contractor was working on ended up being a big disaster. As a result, we ended up having to completely rework his project, at our expense.

After a lot of discussions with the client, they are still with us, and I hope they will be for years, but this guy -- who we hoped to hire for years -- is no longer with us. I can't put all the blame on him, there were communication problems all around, but I didn't think his work was very good.

WEDNESDAY, JANUARY 21, 2005

It's been over two years, and we haven't been able to sell our company, but we were able to buy someone else's business in less than three weeks.

Just five days into the new year, Jack had a meeting with a local web designer, who contacted us when he needed some help with some database programming. It turns out this person was prolific in kicking out what we call "brochure" web sites: Small, static web sites that don't have any interactive components. For example, for a local restaurant he just shows their menu, location, and hours. Because these sites are simple, he's managed to develop over 200 of them in a very short time, but as a result, he was forced to get into the web hosting and email business -- support businesses he doesn't want to be in.

After a few, brief conversations, we bought his hosting and email businesses, and we've already begun moving his customers over to our servers. There's a little mismatch in pricing, as we charge a little bit more than he did, so we may lose some of his customers, but he's already sent out notices to all of his customers telling him what's happening, and letting them know that we monitor the servers and have 24x7 support, and other niceties like email spam filtering.

Our deal was simple: We gave him a very small down payment, and he gets a percentage of the hosting/email revenue for the first year. For a buyer like us, this deal is about as perfect as it gets. Our only risks are the small down payment we gave him, and the cost of one additional server. It creates much more billing work for us, but we think we can automate most of that. It will also increase technical support phone calls, but we hope those will calm down after the initial spike.

While I was skeptical about taking on this business because of the additional support requirements, the other partners felt like we could automate everything, and this could open a new line of business for us. I was finally convinced after (a) talking to everyone who would be taking on additional work, (b) working through the financials, and seeing some profit, and (c) knowing that the recurring revenue would be attractive to potential buyers. We may publicly advertise this as a new service that we offer to clients, but for the time being we just want to absorb these new clients and see how things go for the first few months.

Nothing interesting happened with Marty's ninety-day extension. We did the usual routine of sending information back and forth, but didn't have any meetings with prospective buyers.

With the ninety-day extension expiring, Marty tells me he has another promising lead. He won't give me the name of these people, but he does seem more excited than I've seen him in a while, so after a brief discussion with the other partners, we're going to give him another extension.

While that may not seem like the smartest idea, we just haven't taken the time to look for another business broker, until Jack told me today that he ran into someone he thought we should talk to. As soon as Jack told me the guy's name, I knew who he was. He is well-connected in the area, and knows technology. I've met him briefly twice before, but I didn't come away from those meetings thinking he was a business broker.

Things have moved fast with Marty's new prospect, though not at all in a way I expected. It turns out that they've tried to do some very specialized computer programming work, which is a little different and much more specialized than what they normally do, and they've gotten themselves into a very bad situation.

As a result, we ended up skipping all the preliminary steps, and I spent today working with some of their employees to help dig them out of their hole. I met one of their owners on the way in, but only enough to say hello and exchange brief pleasantries, before I was ushered into their "war room."

Once inside, I learned that they really did dig themselves a deep hole, and it will take me a few days to dig them out. I wish I had known more about the size of this disaster, because this company is located about sixty miles from my home, and I would have gotten a hotel room for a few nights if I'd known how bad it was.

It's hard to describe the situation without giving away anyone's business information, but in short, they've hired some young, inexperienced people you might expect to talk to in a first-level call center, and this is specialized work that involves connecting to a very secure mainframe system. They're used to selling computers and handling routine network work, but they don't have much programming knowledge, and this project is anything but routine.

All their technical people are very nice, and they know they're in way over their heads, and they seem happy to have me there. As long as they don't lose their account with their customer, I should be able to have them limping along tomorrow, with a more permanent fix in place in a few days.

FRIDAY, MARCH 18, 2005

The situation for this client has been stabilized, and everything should be at 100% in the next 48 hours (Saturday or Sunday). They've handcuffed me by not letting me work at the client location, so I've had to do everything remotely. I've never met anyone at their client's location, but from what I've heard on conference calls, the client seems much happier than they were two days ago.

With most of the pressure off now, I took some time to talk to one of the business owners this afternoon. This firm is organized as a corporation, and is owned by two men who I'll guess are in their fifties or sixties. The business owner I've met with so far seems cordial and reasonable, and he seems to be in charge of the technical side of the business. While he seems like a "normal" person in our industry, he warned me that his partner comes across very strongly. He tells me his business partner doesn't mean anything by it, but he's extremely direct and all about the financial numbers, and he said this has a tendency to scare some people off.

Their company is a "full service" computing firm -- beware what you get with a so-called full service computer firm -- nearly three times as large as our company, and as mentioned, they're about sixty miles from Louisville. Their office space is modern and spacious, and I'm told they have another smaller office closer to ours. I've never heard of them, but from the appearances they seem to be doing well.

While waiting in their lobby this morning I picked up some of their marketing material, and found letters of recommendation from their clients, and I know two of these clients very well. I jotted down their names, and I'm trying to think of a good way to ask these clients what they think about this firm.

This afternoon I called Marty to update him on the situation, and also shot an email off to the other partners to let them know things were under control here now. The business partner I've been talking to here seems very happy, so I'm confident I've made a decent impression.

As a side note, seeing this business helps me understand why we have problems growing. From what I've seen, they don't hesitate to hire inexperienced people, which we never do. They're a "general purpose" company that seems very happy to sell you a desktop computer or printer, while we tell people to go to Dell, HP, or some other place when they ask us about buying computers. As a result, I suspect their profit margins are much lower than ours, probably in the 7-10% range, and despite having three times as many employees as we do, I'll guess their net income isn't that much higher than ours.

Jack, Marty, and I met with the two owners of this firm this afternoon, spending nearly three hours in one of their offices. This was a little awkward for me; after working closely with their employees for several days I would have preferred to meet offsite somewhere, but they assured me they would just tell their employees we were discussing other ways of working together.

At the beginning of the meeting they thanked me for helping them out of this jam, and tried to assure us this wasn't their normal way of doing business. I had already filled Jack and Marty in about what happened, and what I thought of their talent level, so I just said we were glad to help, and that their employees had great attitudes about trying to solve problems.

As the first owner ("Good Cop") warned me, his partner ("Bad Cop") was extraordinarily direct, more or less like talking to a computer. I could tell he didn't like small talk, and when I tried to politely say his employees were in over their heads on this project he brushed that statement off, saying they would figure it out and they would be fine. ("Um, sorry buddy," I found myself thinking, "but there were over 1,000 people in my freshman Aerospace Engineering courses, and only 33 of us graduated. Your people were screwed.")

I was sad to see that Bad Cop clearly ran the company, and had only one interest: the bottom line. As we met for nearly three hours, the meeting felt like an interrogation, as if I was a hostile witness in a trial.

As the interrogation went on I kept looking at Good Cop, but he didn't say a word, and often looked down, away from making eye contact with me. Based on this behavior, I felt like he didn't have any balls in their relationship, and I was very disappointed by his complete inaction in this meeting.

Bad Cop was only interested in hard-core financial numbers, and could care less how we did what we did. Jack and I answered all his questions, with the usual reservations that some answers would come after a Letter of Intent. All of this was well-rehearsed by now, and I felt like I was generally giving a speech I've given a dozen times before.

As some questions seemed to open themselves to opportunities to discuss business philosophies, personnel matters, and other "soft" non-financial avenues, I tried to ask questions about their philosophies, but those questions didn't go very far. Good Cop said a few words at these times, but very few, and my impression of him was blown by the third or fourth time I tried this technique, and I finally quit doing anything but directly answering Bad Cop's questions.

It got so bad that I wanted to leave the meeting well before the end of the second hour. Since Jack had already taken a break from the meeting, I decided to do the same thing, and took a bio break, leaving Jack and Marty to answer questions for a while. On the way to the bathroom, and in the bathroom, a couple of employees I had worked with asked me how it was going with Bad Cop. In the bathroom one of the employees looked around to make sure nobody was in the stalls, and told me the good news was that Bad Cop didn't change much; whatever I was seeing in this meeting was pretty much who he is.

I took my time getting back to the meeting, stopping to get a soft drink and saying hello to some of the people I had worked with, but back in the conference room Bad Cop continued his interrogation until I finally snapped. He had a Wendy's drink cup next to his paperwork, so when he again asked another question without even looking at me, I responded to his question with the reply, "Why don't you just buy a Wendy's franchise?"

With that question, Good Cop had a look of horror on his face, but Bad Cop finally stopped, put down his pen, looked at me for a moment, and asked what I meant by that.

Frankly, I can't remember exactly what I told him, but I know that my emotion was that he just kept pushing on the financial numbers, with no interest at all in how we did what we did, or how we had just bailed his company out of a disaster. I had the impression that (a) technology and philosophy were irrelevant to him, and (b) if his company failed on that project and lost that account, it wouldn't have meant anything to him, and this wasn't a person I wanted to work with.

I tried to stay calm on the outside during all of this, but inside I had definitely lost it. It was exactly like you see on television, where a lawyer keeps pushing and pushing until a witness finally cracks, but here it was me that cracked.

Amazingly, he didn't take my comments as badly as I would have expected, and in fact, went right back to his interrogation. When he asked his next question, I turned to Jack, probably with a crazed or stupefied look on my face, and said, "Jack, why don't you take this one?"

At the end of the interrogation Bad Cop asked if we had any questions, and for the first time in a meeting in my career I said "No." I just wanted to leave. This marked one of the few times when I felt true pride in my company, and there was no way I was going to sell my baby to a pure numbers guy.

To my amazement, Jack decided to ask a few questions, maybe to be polite, maybe because he was really interested in something, or maybe just to drive me crazy. I really have no idea what he asked; I started putting my things together, and stood up as soon as one of Jack's questions was answered.

In the parking lot after the meeting Marty asked Jack and I what we thought, and I just said "never," not even giving Jack a chance to reply. Marty said he began to feel the same way when he recently talked to Bad Cop on the phone, but as our agent he was obligated to bring them to the table, and was hoping for something better in person.

Marty called with the "news" that the partners of the company we talked to last week didn't think they were going to make an offer. I'm told I'm normally overly polite with customers and companies that we partner with, often sending them cards, notes, or emails of "thanks," but in this case the thought never occurred to me. I could care less what they thought.

In related news, Marty's second extension with us has run its course, and he asked me if I wanted to renew it. When I asked if he had any new prospects, he said he didn't, so I told him we probably wouldn't renew it, but I would get back to him in a few weeks, but there seemed like no reason to renew it right now. At least I felt he was being honest about when he had prospects and when he didn't.

Jack made contact with the other business broker he met recently, and we met in his office this afternoon. Their office is located in one of the big buildings downtown, with the walls of the room decorated in photos of a "Who's Who" of the local business world.

We met with a man named Steve today, and a simple way to describe Steve is that he reminds me of Mitt Romney in many ways, a tall good looking guy in an expensive suit.

Steve outlined a few ways he thought they could help us. First, they could consult with us on growing our business. Second, they could provide a valuation of our company. Third, they could act as a business broker, the same as Marty, and try to help us sell our company. Interestingly, with the numbers Jack gave him in previous phone conversations, he casually mentioned that our company might be worth $2M, but probably not $3M.

Surprisingly, the consulting agreement strikes me as the most interesting option right now. I've said it before, but my only interest in staying with the company is to try to grow it, and I'm open to some outside advice here. I talked to Jack about this after the meeting, but he's not interested in it, basically saying that he thinks we're doing okay just as we are.

This opened the doors to a little bit of a discussion with Jack about my frustrations in not being able to grow the company, but as I've observed several times recently, he didn't seem to be able to focus on the discussion, so I eventually dropped it.

As we drove down the road, I wondered when the last time was that we had a truly meaningful business discussion. When we first started the company we had some really interesting and deep talks about philosophy, about quality and how we should treat employees and customers, what our marketing material should say, but I can't tell you the last time we've had a conversation like that.

After a long silence, I asked how his wife was doing on some personal things she was pursuing, and he just said "fine."

We met again at Steve's office downtown, and he presented his proposal to us. His first option was that they could consult with us for a surprisingly large fee on how to grow our business. I went in expecting he might want $150 or more per hour for consulting services, but he presented a five-figure *minimum* consulting contract, with no specifics about what they would offer, or even *who* would perform the services. We discussed this for quite some time, and despite my questions, we couldn't get any specific answers. So that five-figure consulting deal isn't going anywhere.

The second option was that they could provide a valuation of our company for a fee of $5,000. That caught me a little by surprise. First, Marty gave us his opinion for free, so I was surprised that someone who might want to sell our company would want to charge us for the right to sell the company. Second, after our previous meeting I was under the impression that he didn't have any professional business valuators on staff, and after asking, indeed they don't. Finally, I reminded him that since he mentioned at our last meeting that our company was probably worth $2M but not $3M, I thought we already had his valuation. He said that was just a ballpark figure, and I told him we were fine with that.

The third option he offered was an agreement similar to Marty's. With no money down, he wanted 10-12% of the sale, depending on the final price. He had checked around, and there was one man in town who was interested in consolidating several computer service firms into one full-service firm, and while they had other firms that were interested in a merger, they didn't have anyone that specialized in an area like we did. He didn't mention the gentleman's name, other than to say he was an older gentleman who had worked in the area before, and he had a good reputation in town. When Steve had his back turned to us, Jack wrote a name on a piece of paper, and slid it over to me. It was the name of the man who Jack guessed Steve was talking about, someone we both knew.

At the end of the meeting, I felt like I wanted to do anything but the status quo, so I was open to the last possibility, though I wasn't completely sold on Steve. It's one thing to see someone's photo in the newspaper, and to hear that he's doing this or doing that, but something altogether different when he won't promise who will do the actual consulting work he's trying to sell us.

I told Steve that Jack and I would discuss this with the other partners, but I didn't see the logic in pursuing his first two offerings. I told him that I was intrigued by the consulting concept, but his five-figure minimum was hard for us to swallow, especially without a guarantee of who would be doing the consulting. I thought this would give him an opportunity to change his stance, or provide more details, but he again refused to get into any specifics, so that option is dead.

I met with all of our business partners today to discuss what we learned from our meetings with Steve. I shared all three of his options, and explained to them why I didn't want to pursue the first two options, and after seeing the costs, they agreed.

As for the third option, everyone has grown a little weary of having the company on the market for so long, and there's no consensus that we should go forward with Steve on that option either. Several partners asked what was so bad about being the size we are. We're all making a very good living, we all like each other, and nobody thinks there's any dead weight at the company.

After what I thought was a good, thorough discussion, we decided not to decide anything today. Frankly, we're all tired, and need our own mental breaks, vacation or otherwise. We'll probably meet again in two weeks.

After the meeting I called Marty and told him we wouldn't be extending his contract, and thanked him for his hard work. From our discussions over the last few years I learned that he likes a particular brand of scotch, and I'm going to the liquor store to pick one up for him. I started to leave a note for my assistant to do this, but that would open up a line of discussion with her I can't have, so I'll do this myself.

And yes, I'm getting one for myself as well.

My wife and I are officially divorced. She's been very nice throughout this entire process, and we came to a settlement about how we'd handle the worth of the company. I may share that here at some point, but right now I don't want to.

There are two things I need to say about a divorce and selling a business though. First, a spouse can make this an incredibly nasty process. As I edit these notes in 2012, it's very easy to point to the recent case of the Los Angeles Dodgers baseball team, and what appeared to be an incredibly nasty, long, drawn-out process between the McCourts. I have no idea what was happening there behind the scenes, but from the outside looking in, it seemed like that case would never end. As my lawyers warned me, any divorce can end up the same way, possibly even forcing a business owner to sell a business he/she doesn't want to sell.

The other thing I'll say is that you have to be very careful with lawyers. I worked with a couple of different ones, and they seem to try to instigate problems where none exist. My wife and I came to agreements on how we wanted to split everything, and then the lawyers got involved, seemingly trying to spin everything, and just made things worse. Fortunately after a while my wife and I sat down, talked about things between ourselves, then agreed to just have the lawyers draw up exactly what we agreed to.

With the divorce finalized, I have to say, there's this thought rumbling around in my head: Why am I still here? Louisville is my wife's hometown, not mine, and while it's a nice enough place to live, I've never really thought of it as home.

I walked to a local bar tonight to have a few drinks. I intentionally didn't drive, this is a "get hammered" night in an effort to put this part of my life behind me. This sounds cliche, but to use a popular phrase, "It is what it is."

During the last three weeks we lost two employees at the company that I care about. I've fired more people than I care to think about, and I've had other employees I didn't really care too much about who quit, but I really cared about these employees.

I always thought we were a decent company to work for, and while we might be a little stale and boring, I do try hard to make it a good place to work. But unfortunately, when you work as a computer programming consultant, you constantly have to work at our customer's office locations, and some of these locations aren't the best. Both of these employees were at less-desirable situations, and not seeing any easy way out, they have left us for other companies.

In a way, I can't say I blame them, but the one thing I would have done in their situations is to come to me (the owner of the business), tell them I couldn't take this particular situation any more, but I wanted to continue working at the firm with another client. But as I've learned over the years, many techies aren't like me, and this was probably too much to expect.

While I cared about the two employees we lost, they were never going to be partners in the LLC, and they weren't project leaders, so we were able to find decent replacements for them, but then a third employee just quit.

This one didn't hurt me as much as the last two, but it still hurt, and in a couple of different ways. First, from a financial standpoint, he did his job, showed up for work every day, and billed at least 1,800 hours every year. He didn't volunteer to work any overtime, but he did his job very well.

He also didn't have a vote of confidence from George. They seemed to get along "okay," but whenever a new project came up for George to run, he never asked for this employee to work with him -- and I do mean *never*. We recently started a new project that George would run, and it would have made for a much shorter commute for this employee, but George said no, he already had some people in mind for the project, even if it meant they had to work a little overtime. I made it clear that this would be a shorter commute for this employee, but it was clear that without me forcing this employee on George, he was not going to work with him. And now that this employee has resigned, I'm not terribly happy with George.

Beyond those two points, it hurts to see three people leave the company in such a short span of time. It has to make other people at the company wonder why everyone is leaving.

After thinking about this a lot, today I made a second offer to buy Jack's shares back from him. I won't say he's completely checked out of our company, but in my opinion his work and behavior is more suited for someone at a much larger company than ours, and I don't think that's a good attitude for a major shareholder and Class A partner to have.

I didn't put anything in writing, but I told him that since we weren't able to sell the company for anywhere near $2M, the company was clearly not worth that. I told him that I'd be glad to buy his shares back on the assumption the company was worth $1.4M, or $14,000 per share (where again, I use the term "share" to mean 1% of the LLC).

I told him he could leave the company if he wanted, or he could stay, but if he stayed, I wanted him to stay in purely a sales role. It didn't have to be commission-based, but I wanted him to just focus on doing what he liked, selling. I even told him I'd be glad if he wanted to keep a smaller ownership in the company, maybe 2-5%.

I tried not to focus on all the negative emotions I felt about him, but instead tried to frame everything in a positive manner, though I did say that he didn't seem happy, and that I wanted to see the old, happier Jack I used to know.

I haven't written a lot of things I've observed about Jack over the last few years, but in my opinion, he is not the same person I started working with all those years ago. Again, I'll skip all those details, other than to say that I've tried to open up some conversations with Jack's wife about this, but she hasn't volunteered anything, and I don't feel comfortable pressing her.

Well, if Jack didn't think I was serious the first time I offered to buy his shares back, today he just didn't take this well at all. He didn't offer to explain himself to me, and generally didn't want to discuss this at all, only saying he wasn't interested in my offer. I told him this was a lot of money, and I wanted him to seriously consider it, but he appeared pretty upset, and abruptly ended the meeting, saying he had another meeting coming up he needed to prepare for.

I do want to say here that I long for the days of our old relationship. I miss the Jack that brought positive energy to the table, the guy that just assumed we were going to do whatever was needed to get things done, and was an all-around great partner.

After making my offer to Jack, and giving him several days to think about it, and nothing coming from it, I have to decide where to go from here with him. I've reviewed the Operating Agreement we casually set up all those years ago, and I'm pretty screwed. With him being a Class A partner, there's no way for me to easily force him out of the company. As I've mentioned, I can buy Class B partners out at book value, but with Class A partners, if you can't agree on a price, you have to get business valuators and lawyers involved.

If it were only Jack, I could try to make his life miserable, but (a) that's not how I like to operate, and (b) with his wife playing an increasingly important role in the company, that's definitely not a winning strategy.

Frankly I'm wondering if I shouldn't be the one to go. While my wife and I have observed that Jack seems more interested in his investments than our business, the truth is that I've been feeling burned out for longer than I can remember.

You know, I try not to swear in this diary, but I hate coming to our #!@% office. Every time I come back to the office there's another project falling apart, or infighting between different groups that I have to work out. A few weeks ago when I was heading out the door for a sales call there was something that had to be done that "only I could do," and I had to run late to that meeting. Again today there were several more near-disasters (technical problems), and everyone pounced on me before I could even set my laptop bag down.

David tells me there's very clear tension between several people in the office, and it would be best if I was at the office more often to serve as a go-between for them. That's great, I tell David, except for the fact that I still have all these projects in the field that I'm responsible for. I understand that David doesn't like to get involved in these things, and he's also not at the office much, but Jack and George are at the office all the time, so why the heck can't they deal with these things, or even let me know these problems exist?

With my problems with Jack, I didn't do much to keep my composure with him or George. I called them both into our conference room, and thin walls or not, ripped into them for not handling things at the office. I told them they were business partners, and they had to take care of these things. I told them I'm sorry I'm not here in the office, I have to work out in the field to manage these projects, they're here in the office, and they need to handle these things, and avoiding problems is not handling them.

After a calming down period, I've talked to each employee and partner who seem to be involved in the problems, both so I can understand what's happening, as well as to let them vent. In response to some of their complaints, I'm investing money in a technical solution to some of the problems -- things nobody brought to my attention before -- and I'm also trying to do a few things to help with the softer side of the problems.

To that end, we're going to bring on another contractor to help lessen everyone's workload. We're not going to charge much for this person's time, and this is going to cost us more money than we'll make, but it will hopefully clear up the technical/workflow portions of the problems.

We're also going to start having a few more company outings, including lunch outings, and various training programs. These programs are non-technical, and in fact, have very little to do with work directly. Frankly, they're just an excuse for a boondoggle, to get the employees together in a fun or learning situation with less pressure.

All of this will be on the company's dime, and if I haven't explained Jack and George's personalities very well yet, suffice it to say they're not happy with this at all. In a partner meeting today I told them I appreciate their criticism, but if they didn't like my approach, what I would really appreciate is a better solution, especially since they're both in the office all the time, and I'm not.

Neither one could offer a better solution, only saying they think the problems are overblown. When they said that, I took the time to explain exactly what I feel every time I walk in the office, telling them that I can't even set my laptop bag down on my desk before someone is on top of me with the latest disaster.

This motivational talk from me didn't seem to help anything, and everyone seemed to clam up, so I closed the meeting by telling everyone that I'm open to other suggestions, but lacking a better plan at this time, this is the way we're going.

David knew I was boiling over, and called me later in the evening to see how I was doing, and to help talk me down, but I wasn't in any mood to be talked down, and just said "Fuck them." I wrote David much later in the evening to apologize for my language and behavior, but he said it was okay, we all need to vent sometimes. He also said I was right, nobody was offering a better solution.

Thursday, June 30, 2005

Today was the first "social" engagement I set up for everyone at the company. The employees that attended the event said they enjoyed it, and offered ideas for what we should do for our next event. Several employees couldn't make it to the engagement, most notably Jack and George. So much for "business partners" helping to build any team spirit.

After the gathering I sent an email to the other partners telling them the engagement seemed to go well, and employees had ideas for our next gathering. I wrote that I was disappointed that several of them couldn't make it, and I hoped they would be at the next gathering. I then added that I was going out of town for a few days to try improve my own mental state in regards to our company.

While I'm out of town, Marty called and told me he's just checking in to see how things are going. I told him I'm having a great time on a short vacation in California, and that we don't currently have the company on the market with anyone else.

He told me that it looked like Rob was going to be coming back into the scene with a stronger offer than before, but then his employer offered him a chance to work on a job in Europe, and he and his wife are on their way out of town. Good for him, but bad for me; I should have gone back to him at some point to see if he wanted to work with us.

Marty thanked me for the bottle of scotch again, and we both bemoaned the inability to sell the company before hanging up.

Shortly after his call, I got a phone call from a woman who sounded frantic, with a blaring siren in the background. I had to keep yelling that I couldn't hear her, but after a little while I finally realized it was the woman he cleaned our offices once a week. She had accidentally set off the fire alarm, and although I have no idea how she knew my cellphone number, I was the one she called. As we spoke, I could hear the fire engines showing up at the office. I eventually spoke to some people from the fire department, and got things straightened out as much as possible.

Such is the life of a small business owner.

I spoke with David and Jack last week about selling more ownership to several other key employees. We have several other employees besides George and Cooper that have been very solid contributors for the last five years, and I thought they at least deserved a shot. Whether or not they can afford it is something else, but I thought we should at least discuss their candidacy.

Based on everything we've learned in the process of trying to sell the company, it's clear that the price I've offered in the past was a really great deal for those shares. The company hasn't changed significantly since the last time I sold any shares, and I sold them then for $4,500 for every 1% share. The partners who bought at that price got their money back very fast, so I'm looking at a higher price, maybe as much as $12K to $14K per share, in part based on my last offer to Jack.

I checked this with Jack and David, and they said it was probably a little high for employees buying into becoming partners, and something more like $6K to $8K per share might be good for partners buying in, but in either case, they doubted anyone I wanted to offer it to could afford it.

Besides these other employees, I'm finally going to offer a little more ownership to Cooper. He's asked for this several times, and with everything going on, I've been very slow in getting back with him.

I should also mention that I didn't tell David about my recent offer to buy Jack's shares back from him. I'd love to tell David about it, he's been a great partner and friend, but it doesn't seem appropriate.

I had a meeting with all the business partners today, both Class A and B, and brought up the idea of offering ownership interest to several other employees who I thought had become key employees.

George was opposed to offering interest to all the technical people, but was slightly more open to offering a small amount of ownership to our lead designer. He said he didn't think one employee could afford it at all, and said, "Why bother offering it to him?"

I also announced that I was offering a little more ownership interest to Cooper, though I hadn't set a price on those shares yet. I said I appreciated his contributions to the company, and had always intended to offer him more. At that time, nobody complained to me, but I could tell from the look on George's face that he wasn't happy about this.

Partner issues

If I haven't mentioned it before, in my opinion, Jack and George are the two most money-driven people I've ever met. I'm not saying there's necessarily anything wrong with their approach to money, or that there aren't many other people who deal with money the way they do, it's just very different from my approach.

At this point I could care less what they do in their personal lives, but when it comes to making business decisions they always seem to take the short-term view of money -- like suggesting we lay some people off when business was slower after the dot-com bubble and again in 2002 -- and I can't allow that.

I mention this because by offering more ownership to Cooper, I seem to have really upset George. He came to me after the meeting to air his complaints, but as I tried to explain to him, way back when he was first made a business partner, I told him I was hoping to have a group of other business partners with 5-10% ownership shares, and I didn't want to go higher than 10% for any individual, unless the partners made some purchases between each other. He still wasn't happy, but this was the truth then, and it still is.

I also finally told him that the issues he's had with customers have been holding him back from being a Class A partner. I've told him that I've wanted to talk to him about this for a long time, but Jack had been telling me to avoid the situation, but now I felt like it really needed to be said. "We're a consulting firm," I said, "you can't just keep pissing off customers." I'm sure this didn't make him feel any better, but I had to put this ownership issue in perspective, and it was also driving me crazy not to say anything about this for so long.

Getting back to the meeting, as angry as I've been with everyone lately, I was almost floored when the partners noted as a group that if I was interested in selling any more interest to them, they would like to buy more, though they'd appreciate it if I lowered the asking price from $12K down to something like $6K to $9K. They said they understood where I was coming from with the $12K number, but it seemed like the number should be lower for them.

Jack didn't say anything during this discussion, and it burned me up that only he and I knew that I had recently offered $14K for each of his shares.

I just got back into town today after going home to the Chicago area to celebrate a relative's 75th birthday. The party was fun, but truthfully, I just wanted to get out of town again for a few days. Since the divorce, I've been thinking more and more about what's keeping me in Kentucky, and on this trip I finally came to the decision that there's *nothing* that's keeping me here. Nothing, that is, except the business.

Since coming to that decision, I keep thinking about how I can get out of the business, as in, "Screw the partners, how can *I* get out of here." In this state of mind, I've thought about selling all my interest in the business, either to my partners or perhaps to an outside entity, maybe someone like Steve, Jerry, or even our closest competitors in town. On the trip back to Kentucky today I decided that one way or another I'm going to make this happen. I'll do whatever I have to do sell the entire company, or just sell my shares in the company so I can get out of here.

I hate to say it, but I'm currently thinking about taking this to an extreme, about putting my client's projects on the back burner, and making the process of selling my interest in the company my number on priority. Until now I've really on Marty to do all that work, but now I just want to take things into my own hands.

I'll list all my reasons for making this decision at some point, but I've written about the major ones already, including feeling burned out, the inability to grow the company, constantly having to deal with Jack and George, and knowing that this is not my hometown, and not the town I want to retire in.

Liberating decision

It may seem ridiculous as you read this, but just making this decision feels incredibly liberating. The simple act of making this decision in my mind that come hell or high water, I'm going to sell my shares and get on with my life ... I've felt an insane energy rush. During the long drive back here I could hardly sit still in the car, and now as I write this at almost four in the morning, I still don't have any plans to go to sleep tonight.

You know what they say about a monkey being lifted off your back? It feels just like that, except instead of a monkey it's like a two-ton weight has been lifted, and I feel as light and energetic as I've felt since being about 22 years old. The worst part of this great buzz was wasting it while sitting in the car. I kept wishing I was playing basketball or football in the park, or out on a beach somewhere.

What's really blowing me away right now is that just a simple thought like this can make me feel so good. I haven't even sold my interest, I've just made the mental commitment to take things in my own hands and get this done, and those thoughts alone make me feel like this? That's crazy. Has work really been draining me this much? I knew I wasn't happy, but I didn't realize what a burden the company had become.

At this crazy hour of the morning I have to admit that I'm probably not thinking straight, but my current plan is to get out of here by late spring of next year, maybe early summer, and head up to Alaska. My wife and I first went up there back in 2001, and I instantly fell in love with the area, and after recently re-watching the movie *Insomnia*, it instantly popped into my mind that's where I should go.

Well, for now, that's just dreaming. The first thing I have to do is to get out of here. Actually, the *first* thing I have to do is tell everyone else that one way or another, I'm leaving.

WEDNESDAY, AUGUST 3, 2005

After writing that last entry, I wrote a longtime friend of mine to tell him of my "decision," and how I feel. Here's part of what I wrote:

"I haven't been able to make any strides towards growing the company, and frankly, every day I have to psych myself into thinking I want to be there.

I don't know if it makes any sense, but I actually 'quit' in my mind on the drive home, and just that thought of quitting has given me an incredible buzz."

Here are a few excerpts from his reply:

"Huh, made up your mind finally? LOL!

I'm sure that after the separation and divorce this must have crossed your mind quite strongly. Very good that you used time to show you what you needed to know.

Certainly you have something in mind for what comes next, or will in time. I am sure that whatever it will be, it is what's driving this decision. It would be a shame if this was just to get out from under something dealing w/ the divorce or business problems. Meaning that yes, profitability is important, yet keeping the business viable for those who rely on it is a responsibility of sorts. However you can't tie your life to it in a way that impinges on your quality of life."

He's a pretty philosophical sort, and I've never really thought about my responsibility to keep people employed. I guess I have, and of course made the decision back in 2002 to keep everyone employed, even at my own expense. But beyond that, I always thought our employees were good enough that with just a few phone calls I'd have them all employed somewhere else, so that never stressed me out much.

After not sleeping the other night, I decided that I need to let this idea settle in for a little while, and make sure that this is what I really want to do. I've already spent a long time thinking about this, and I'm pretty sure this is what I want to do, but once I announce my decision to leave by next spring, that's not something I'll be able to take back easily.

As I look back at my own notes, the one thing that stands out is my comment that I don't want to retire in this town. There's nothing wrong with it, it's just not my hometown, and the longer I think about that, it seems like a waste of time to live here any longer.

I gave my decision to sell my interest in the business another week to settle down, to weigh the pros and cons, and also look at the financial aspects of this decision.

The most important part of this is the financial part. I crunched all the numbers, and even if I could magically sell my interest for $12K per share, I don't think I'll have enough money to retire on, especially if I really do want to buy a home somewhere and settle down. So that's very important, this is clearly not a "sell and retire" move.

At this point I also don't know what I'd want to do for work after the sale. I'm going to give myself time on this one, though, as I have a few ideas, and in the worst case, I just go back to what I'm doing already, perhaps on my own. I don't dislike the work; I just feel beat down by running this company.

I'm also very anxious to move on, and frankly I can't fight that feeling. A few years ago I bought a motorcycle, and the idea of touring the country on a cycle is also rumbling around in my head. My current thoughts are to sell my interest in the company for whatever I can, with the understanding that I'll be leaving by early summer, earlier if possible.

To say the least, it's been hard to concentrate on my business projects lately. If I thought Jack had already mentally checked out, well, he's got nothing on me.

I told my wife, er, former wife, of my plans, that I want to sell my shares for whatever price I can get and then leave as soon as possible, and that I'm going to tell the other partners very soon. I'm telling her because she's still a friend, probably my best friend, and because I don't want this to cause a problem for her at the office. I suggested that she might want to move to a different company, or do whatever she wanted to follow her own interests, but that's up to her.

Her response was funny in a way. She said she was shocked by the suddenness of it, but also said she knew it was coming. I told her I was glad she knew that, and wished she had told me about it a few months ago. We hugged, and I left.

SATURDAY, AUGUST 13, 2005

I sent another email to my friend back in the Chicago area a little while ago, and it sums up my feelings at the moment very well:

"The weird part about owning a biz is that you can't just leave. Well, you can, but you'd have to forfeit a lot of money, which I don't want to do right now. So the next step is working out an agreeable exit for me, either with the current partners, or an outside entity who would either want to (a) buy the entire company, (b) just buy my shares, or (c) buy a portion of my shares while the current partners buy the other shares.

It's hard to know if this is exactly the right thing to do, but for a while I have definitely felt like an athlete who knows they should retire, but they stay around a little too long.

I read some Carlos Castaneda books in college, and I remember him writing about having 'death as a friend that is always looking over your shoulder.' I don't think it was meant to be a morbid thing, but a thoughtful thing, something to make sure your actions are honorable, something like that. I have a Samurai book (*Hagakure*) and they mention a similar thing. It's supposed to be a good thing that Death is always there w/ you, asking things like 'If you die tomorrow will you be happy?'

So yesterday I turned and asked Death if I should stay, but he only said 'What do you think?' Not much help there. :)

There's also a concept of a 'tombstone test', meaning 'When you die what do you want to have written on your tombstone?' Being a successful business owner isn't anywhere on that list for me.

I also have this feeling that as a consultant, I'm always solving other people's problems, and I'm burned out on that. I'd love to be able to create something of my own, not for the money, but to create something really great, like a piece of art that stands the test of time. It doesn't have to be the most awesome thing in the world, but just a little something that has a positive impact on a few lives, or who knows, many lives.

Finally, I also don't want to be the guy that 'Hung around just to get a good paycheck'. I *really* don't like people like that, people that retire long before they leave."

He wrote back several things of interest, which he's allowed me to share here:

"You've written, 'If you die tomorrow will you be happy?' and '... try to do one thing that's truly great, by myself, something like art ... and I'd like to be able to say that I did something like that.'

Certainly a good question, and a terrific goal. I feel that if you have a vision of this goal and the bug has got you ... go ahead and start taking the steps. Having a vision of this goal and living towards it ... becomes like serendipity. You fulfill yourself and the goal at the same time.

Really how awesome is that? I believe you can do it, no matter that the final design is unknown at this point. Doing this also answers that first question for you.

I do believe however you can die happy w/o something like this happening in life. That would be quite a discussion however, lol."

It sure is helpful to have someone to share these thoughts with. I know I can go a little berserk sometimes, but this friend has always been there for me, and I really do appreciate that.

Sunday, August 14, 2005

It's early on the morning of Monday, August 15th, but since I haven't gone to sleep yet, I'm putting this entry under Sunday the 14th.

I have a favorite Mexican restaurant nearby, and I love sitting in the bar area there. I usually eat some type of appetizer, and have a couple of margaritas, and because they've had the same wait staff there forever, I've gotten to know several of the people there a little bit. I guess it's my version of the bar from the tv series Cheers.

I went there tonight, and ended up talking to one of the waitresses about some of my thinking. She knows I own a company, so I just jumped in and told her I was wondering what it would be like to sell the company, and find a job that I liked, and supposing I could only make $30K or $40K at that job, I wondered if I could be happy with that.

She slapped me in the face with the reality of her reply: "Honey, I don't even make $30K, so you're asking the wrong person." When I left, I left her a big, fat tip, and she gave me a hug on the way out.

I told the Class A partners I had to meet with them as soon as possible, not telling them what the meeting was about, and we arranged to meet at the office thirty minutes after closing time. It's sad to say about my own company, but thirty minutes after five o'clock you don't have to worry about running into too many employees. There was just one employee there, a guy named Eric that I wanted to make a partner offer to that George doesn't seem to like, and he left just as we got around to starting the meeting.

Before inviting the Class A partners to this meeting, I debated about whether I should tell the A and B partners the news at the same time, or just tell the Class A partners first. I finally decided to tell the Class A partners about my decision first. Part of this is a legal matter going back to the Operating Agreement: If I offer my shares for sale, they have the right of first refusal, meaning they can buy them before the Class B partners even have a chance.

Because David is still a good friend (while Jack and I rarely speak), I thought about telling him first, but I told them the news at the same time. There wasn't much to say, and to my own surprise it was easy to say:

"I called this meeting to announce that I plan to leave this company and this town no later than early next summer, and my entire ownership in the company is now for sale for. We've talked recently that the company may be worth $12K per share, and seeing that whoever buys my interest will have controlling interest in the company, the shares may be worth even more.

You need to read our Operating Agreement, but my understanding is that as Class A partners, you have the first option to buy these shares, so I'm offering them to you first. According to our bylaws you have thirty days to make a decision to buy them or not, at which point I can make them available to the Class B partners."

Jack and David's initial reaction seemed to be shock, perhaps in the bluntness of my approach, but David eventually said he thought this would happen when he learned that my wife and I were separated. (Again, someone telling me this would have been helpful.)

David asked a lot of questions like "Why?" and "Are you sure?", and I answered them as much as I felt like saying with Jack in the room. The truth is, David and Eric are my only friends at the company, guys I'll stay in touch with after I leave, so other than them, I didn't think my reasons were anyone else's business. However, I made it clear that my wife had nothing to do with my decision, other than that being married to her was what brought me to this town in the first place.

At this point -- there's no other way to say it -- I lied, and told them I had several people outside the company that might be interested in buying my shares, but that I had to follow the bylaws of our Operating Agreement. I told them I'd rather sell to all of the current partners, but if we couldn't work something out, that I also thought these other people could afford to buy my interest, but probably not the entire company. I told them this was why I had already looked at the Operating Agreement, and knew about the thirty-day terms.

By the end of the meeting, it seemed like David and Jack had absorbed what I told them, and while I don't know how they were feeling, I felt great. Shoot, I was ready to hop in the car and drive off into the sunset, but unfortunately I still had to stay; there was this little matter of selling my ownership before I left. I knew I wanted to leave as soon as I could, but I also didn't want to walk away from at least a six-figure deal before I left.

Before the meeting was over we decided to get in touch with the company lawyer, to make sure we all understood the ground rules we needed to follow during this process. I had read enough of the Operating Agreement that I knew I needed to talk to the Class A partners first, but I wasn't completely sure about what to do after that, and of course this was all a surprise to them, so I assumed they hadn't read the agreement in some time.

I'm finally trying to take the time to list the thoughts behind my decision-making process, so here goes.

First, again, this isn't my hometown, and I don't want to retire here.

Second, as a consultant, I'm tired of working on projects for other people. One of my real strengths as a technical consultant has been my empathy for my customers, and over the last two years, I've felt that slipping away. Besides whatever intelligence I have, I always thought my superpower was that I cared more about the success of projects than even my customers did, and now that had faded away. Projects were no longer "life or death" matters for me.

Third, with only one exception, I've always been responsible for the largest projects at the company, and going back to the previous paragraph, I don't want to tackle any more large projects right now. Call it burnout or whatever, but that's the way I feel.

Fourth, as I wrote earlier, every time I come back to the office, I feel like I'm walking into a disaster area. How things get done here on a daily basis, well, I can only guess.

Fifth, my relationship with Jack has deteriorated to the point that a "divorce" from him is an extremely welcome thing. While it would be a negative thing for me to have to stay here and work with him any longer, the truth is I don't have to see him much, and this item is only fifth on my list of reasons.

Sixth, as I've written several times, not having any success at growing the company over the last few years has made the company boring and stagnant. It's my opinion that the other partners seem to have a very limited interest in growing the company, and staying the same size holds zero interest for me any more.

Finally, as I wrote in the email to my friend, I know there are still some computer/technical things I still want to pursue, something I want to create, so I know I'm not completely burned out, hopefully I'm just burned out on other people's problems for the time being.

In trying to be really truthful with myself, there are also several things about my current personal situation I'm not happy with that have very little to do with this company or this town:

First, I'm not eating well, and I'm not taking care of my body. While this town seems to put little to no emphasis on a healthy lifestyle (compared to cities in California, Arizona, Colorado, etc.), I still have to accept that I can eat better and join a gym. I do work a lot, but I need to take a hard look at that versus my health.

Second, I don't feel any room for creative expression at the company. Because I'm the owner, and I also run all the large projects, it's always about the current project, and everything else that comes with owning the company. I'm sure this sounds like I'm a control freak, but if you could ask the people that work with me, they'll say I'm not. But to me, all of this is a huge investment of time, and I don't feel like I'm "growing" at all. It's like always doing the "meatball surgery" they talk about on M*A*S*H.

I'm in my forties, and I feel like I should be more mature emotionally, but frankly, at this time, I really just don't care. I've given so much time into building this business, and, okay, if I'm burned out, I'm burned out.

I've taken some time to makes notes regarding the terms of our Operating Agreement as they apply to a business partner leaving the company. Because I had no idea what I was doing when I converted the company to an LLC, I went with a boilerplate agreement, the kind you can easily find on the internet these days, so there aren't any secrets here.

David, Jack, and I are still going to meet with our company attorney, but at least 90% of the Operating Agreement is easy to read, if not boring, so I worked through it myself. Here's an overview of what the agreement says about a business partner that wants to leave, with a few of my own notes thrown in:

- Class A members have all management and voting rights; Class B members have no management or voting rights, just rights to distributions.
- A 75% supermajority is required to authorize the Company to repurchase Membership Units. (Presumably a 75% vote among Class A members, not including myself, because I am the seller.)
- There's a one year non-competition agreement that prohibits the selling member to talk to "existing or prospective" clients. This is for a one year period from the date he sells his interests.
- There are some events that trigger termination of a member's interest, including retirement (is that me?), voluntary resignation (definitely me), breach, bankruptcy, divorce decree transfers, and death.
- The section that details how a "terminating member's units" will be valued, and it gets a little dicey here:

  - Class A Membership Units Valuation Price = Fair Market Value

  - Class B Membership Units Valuation Price = Lesser of Net Book Value or Capital Account Balance (if purchased within 3 years of acquiring), or Fair Market Value (if purchased more than 3 years after acquiring)

- In determining *Market Value*, the parties can either (a) Make a value determination internally, or (b) Each party (Company or Member as Buyer, and terminated Member as Seller) hires an independent appraiser to determine the value within 30 days, and if the appraisers cannot come to a mutual decision, you average the two numbers to come to a final value.

- If the Company decides not to purchase a terminated Member's Units, and all the Class A Members (Jack, David) also decide not to purchase, the Class B Members (George, Cooper) have the right to purchase their pro rata shares.

- With regard to terms of payment for the Units, if the Purchaser is another Member, the purchase price must be paid in full at Closing. If the Purchaser is the Company, 25% must be paid up front, with the remaining amount paid over 2 years with interest at prime +1%.

- Upon the occurrence of a "triggering event" (presumably me saying I'm leaving), a terminated Member (me) has the right, for a 30 day period, to purchase any insurance policies owned by the Company or another Member on his life for the interpolated terminal reserve plus a proportionate part of the gross premium last paid before date of transfer.

- No Member can sell his/her interest in the Company without first offering it to the Company and the remaining Members at the value stated above (Fair Market Value or Net Book Value). Upon receiving a written offer for purchase, the remaining Members have 30 days to decide whether they will purchase, or the Company will purchase, or neither. If they decide not to purchase, the Member can sell to a third party.

In summary, I'm a Class A Member, and the value of the shares of a Class A Member are "fair market price," which, to me, is currently $12K per share.

That being said, however this works out, I hope we can agree to a price without having to pay for two valuators. It seems obvious that Jack would try to get a valuator to say the company is worth $1, and

I'd try to get someone who would say the value is clearly $12K per share, or using Marty's initial estimate, about $50K per share.

As I've noted before, the Class B Member shares aren't worth very much. From everything I've read, *book value* is essentially fire sale value, and this isn't a fire sale, we're a very healthy company, at least financially.

It's Saturday evening now, and I'm just catching up on the events of the last few days. My friend wrote today to ask how the meeting went with the business partners the other day. Here's my reply:

"Well, I hope things will work out okay, I don't know. I already see some problems, but hopefully it won't implode. Jack canceled several meetings and seems to be running around, presumably talking to lawyers, and wants to immediately know exactly how much I want, etc.

Did I mention that I told them I thought I had some potential outside investors willing to buy my interest? That was pretty much just a lie at the time, but really, I do know a couple of people who might have enough money and interest to buy my shares ... time will tell.

I know I should have put more thought into this process, but I really just wanted to get the ball rolling so I can get out of town as early as possible next year.

One thing that's funny is that within the last month we agreed that we should offer shares of the company to a few employees, and we agreed to a certain price range for those shares. (That is, I'd be selling my shares to these employees.) But now that the tables are turned, Jack keeps coming up with all these reasons why that exact same price range is not only too high, but way too high. Funny how that works (not).

I'm meeting w/ my main partner Class A partners and the company lawyer on Tuesday to review a document known as our 'Operating Agreement.' As mentioned, Jack seems to have gone into panic mode, and wanted to meet with the lawyer today, but I told him that was ridiculous, there was no way I was going to pay a lawyer overtime to discuss this, and I suggested he read the Agreement himself, it's not too hard to read. I also told him I'm not leaving right now, that I fully plan to stay here until the end of spring at the earliest.

The crazy thing is that he seems to be panicking, and I'm sitting here working on my vacation plans for next spring. I'd love to start with a long motorcycle ride. I mentioned this to David, and he gave me a copy of 'Zen and the Art of Motorcycle Maintenance,' which talks about a long motorcycle vacation trip."

He wrote back:

"Dude, consider that book to be a metaphor, lol. The trip may be real, and I think the actual itinerary is well-documented on the internet, but as far everything else, keep your mind open ... :)"

David, Jack, and I met at the office of our company lawyer this afternoon. The truth is, we've barely needed a lawyer so far for anything but basic employee and customer agreements, and I don't know him very well. He's never really impressed me, but we haven't needed him much, so it hasn't been a problem.

The three of us arrived at the lawyer's office together, all coming in from different directions. It felt weird, sneaking out of my client site (again) without telling anyone where I was going. One person did ask, and I said I had a doctor's appointment, which I planned to tell everyone.

I learned at this meeting that I don't care for our lawyer. He seems "slippery," and talks for a long time without really saying anything, and also talks way too much for someone that gets paid by the hour. I had to interrupt him constantly just to get to the point.

I had my business Operating Agreement notes with me, and he basically echoed those. He clarified the "75% supermajority" term, saying that since I was leaving, my ownership didn't count in this vote, and it was 75% of whoever was remaining.

This part of the agreement was also interesting, because it meant the "company" could agree to buy my shares, and then those shares would cease to exist. The ownership in the company would then be based on the ratio of outstanding shares. In this case the "company" would be Jack and David, as they would be the remaining Class A business partners. So, if Jack and David -- acting as the company -- can agree with me on a sales price, I can sell my interest to "the company."

We also got one other important piece of information from the lawyer. It turns out that he can't help either of us individually, he can only represent "the company." He said that I needed to get my own lawyer, and anyone interested in buying my shares should also get their own lawyers. If and when we have agreed to the terms of a deal, he can write up the business sales documents from a company perspective, but other than that, there isn't anything he can do for us individually. Considering that he struck me as such a slippery character today, I can actually respect that position.

Jack and I are going to meet for lunch tomorrow to discuss my leaving, what I want, etc., so I'm trying to work up some specific terms tonight. Unfortunately David can't make it to lunch, which is a real shame, because he's a real calming influence for us.

The biggest thing at the moment is trying to honestly figure out what the company is worth without me. We've had the business on the market for several years now, and haven't been successful trying to sell it. We had one offer for $1.4M (with some really bad buyout terms), so "fair market value" for the business is clearly less than that.

When I recently talked to the partners about me selling more of my shares to other employees, I floated the idea of $12K per share, and while the other partners agreed that price seemed reasonable for outside buyers, they hoped I would offer my shares for less to employees, so that's another price point.

Arguably some factors that make my shares less valuable now are (a) I'm leaving the company, and a large portion of the company revenue runs through my projects, and (b) I want to leave by early next summer, only nine to ten months from now.

I don't really know how to judge the minimum values my shares are worth. I know Jack will argue that the company is worth less without me, but since we haven't do much selling or marketing lately (mostly just responding to incoming phone calls and servicing existing clients), that argument doesn't hold too much for me. That being said, we've clearly gotten several deals because of my relationships and work in previous sales meetings, and with George's seeming history of rocky relationships with clients, there is some truth here, though I won't admit to it.

I've finally decided to just share some of my thinking with Jack tomorrow, and see how he responds. I won't say that $12K/share is exactly what I want, just that it clearly seems to be the high end, and we need to figure out where to go from there.

Jack and I met at lunch today, and he surprised me in two ways, none of them good.

First, without even knowing the price, he said he had no interest in buying my shares in the company, and wouldn't go along with any effort by David to pursue that. That wasn't a huge surprise; I'm not sure exactly why, but I didn't think he'd go for that approach anyway. However, his second surprise was more like a shock.

He said he wanted to make a counteroffer to me: He wanted to sell his interest in the company for some percentage over book value back to me. Not much he said, maybe twenty or thirty percent.

To this, my response was pretty much something like this: "You son of a bitch. Let's see, I already tried to buy your shares twice, I've been divorced, I've already stated that I want to leave town, and then you do this? What a piece of shit." (Actually, what I said was even worse than that, I just tried to clean it up here a little bit.)

For some reason I tried to sit there with him after this, but I couldn't. I told him that if he wanted to read the Operating Agreement and follow the correct protocol by making an offer to sell his interest to the company, that was his prerogative, but in my opinion, I thought that would make him look like an ass to David and all the other partners who would soon learn the truth.

As I said that I got up and left, not even thinking about the bill. We had ordered some food, but it hadn't arrived, and I didn't care. What I did care about a little while later was that I was really hungry, and I had to go back to a client site to work on a project. I stopped at McDonalds on the way back to the site, got a burger, and ate it on the drive back.

I was clearly still upset when I got to the client site, and when I ran into David he asked what was going on. We closed the door to our working area at our client site, and I told him what happened at lunch. He didn't get a chance to say much though, because some customers came by, and we had to quit talking about this, but he quickly suggested I get out of there, which I did.

It's late at night now, I'm still very upset, and I wrote my friend about this. He wrote back:

"Is this the guy you mentioned that checks on his investments during the day? Here's how I see it: He sees the end of the gravy train, and he wants to bail out before you do. How much revenue do you think you generate for the company? 20%? 50%? Whatever it is, he sees much less revenue when you leave. Also, he may be trying to set you up to reduce your asking price."

I'm so pissed right now, it's ridiculous. It's hard to believe I have been "business partners" with this person.

Since I have a ton of energy in this current state of rage ... for the record, "book value" is an incredibly misleading number for a transaction like this. Book value can fluctuate wildly, depending on how much cash you have in the bank. We've got $500K in cash in the bank right now, but let's say we take a $300K distribution. Book value was $500K, but now it's $200K. Book value is a meaningless number, especially in a service business, where we don't have a bunch of equipment to sell off.

I've read four books on selling a business in the last several years, and they all stress that book value is "fire sale value," meaning that you're going out of business and just trying to dump the company. Our business isn't anything like that, in fact everyone that sees the financial reports calls it a "cash cow."

Earlier this evening I sent Jack an email and cc'd David, summarizing our "discussion" that he won't agree to buy my interest when acting on behalf of the company, and that he's also interested in selling his shares to the company. I'm trying to keep things legal, so I feel like I need something in writing, essentially leaving a paper trail with emails. So I sent him this email, which he hasn't replied to yet.

Assuming he replies that he won't agree to buy my shares while acting on behalf of the company, I then have to make an offer to these same two guys acting individually. Assuming they won't want to buy my shares individually, and also assuming Jack won't also try to sell his shares at the same time, I can then make an offer to George and Cooper, the current Class B partners.

To keep everything rolling along I'd like to be able to do that tomorrow, but depending on how much of a jerk Jack wants to be, he can technically delay the company's decision thirty days, and then delay his Class A partner decision thirty days, but I don't think he'd dare do that. If he did that, David will know immediately what has happened, and Cooper and George will also know in sixty days, and he'll look like a fool.

SUNDAY, AUGUST 28, 2005

Two days later, and I'm still very upset with Jack. He hasn't called or written, and at this moment I have no plans of ever talking to the man again, unless I have to for some business reason. Even then, we certainly can't go on sales calls together any more. If I thought I was upset with him over the last few years, that pales in comparison to what I think of him right now.

My problems with Jack

There are a lot of things I haven't written here about Jack, because I didn't want to get into it too much, but before I made my last offer to buy his shares, I made a list of all my reasons for doing that. All of this is just my opinion, but it may give you an idea of my problems with Jack as a business partner from my perspective:

- I don't think he wants to be a salesperson any more.
- He's supposed to be the sales and marketing person, but doesn't seem open to ideas on marketing. I spent time working on marketing ideas with David, Cooper, and our other salesperson, and he did nothing with those ideas.
- He hasn't shown up at our most recent technical seminars, and hasn't followed up with any prospects after these seminars.
- He doesn't seem to want to hire good salespeople to work for him. On the technical side, we only hire people that are clearly better than I am, but he constantly hires inferior salespeople who don't work out, and seems upset when I recommend good people I know. (This isn't a huge problem, as we can't seem to hire other good technical talent, but more sales would at least push us harder to find other people, and maybe we'd figure out how to train and work with those people.)
- He's done nothing to support the events we tried to put together to improve company morale.

To the point of not hiring good salespeople, even David mentioned this to me recently. He asked why we don't hire better salesperson, and after a few moments I couldn't think of much else to say other than "That's a hell of a good question."

None of this matters too much any more, as I just want to leave, but Jack looks like he's going to create some real problems here, especially if he does want to repeat his offer to sell his shares this week.

A business sales price I think is fair

Given that Jack is pushing the situation, I decided to work harder to figure out what price I think is "reasonable" for my shares, especially considering that I want to leave by early summer.

To summarize what I've written, there are several ways to look at potential prices for the company, including:

- Rob's offer.
- Not receiving any other offers at our asking price.
- The back of the envelope $2M estimate that Steve gave us.
- Our business broker's discretionary cash flow technique.
- Book value, which I think is a worthless measure.

The company may be worth less with me gone, especially since most large projects and sales efforts do involve me, but to think that they'd lose that much business isn't right. The truth is that David can now run a project as well as I can, so he simply replaces me in that role, and they hire to back-fill his current role.

The bigger impact of my leaving might be to future sales, but that's where the existing so-called partners need to step up, especially George. Shoot, he just told me he wants to buy more shares, well, it looks like he's about to get one heck of an opportunity there.

The wildcard here is whether Jack is going to formally make an offer to sell his shares, and if and when he does that, when the whole story comes out, it will be clear to everyone that I can't work with him any more.

Still no word from Jack today, and from my end, I have no interest in talking to the man unless I need to respond to something. I've already decided that George needs to go on all future sales calls with Jack.

It may not sound like much here, but I've reaffirmed my commitment to be very aggressive about selling my business interest, even if it takes sacrificing the quality of my work, or anything else I normally do for the company. If/when George or Cooper call with a problem, I'll just say, "Deal with it, I'm too busy." That's never been how I've approached business, but it's how I do it now.

Step 1 is that I need to find a good lawyer. I made some calls first thing this morning, and I have three appointments in the next two days. I'll use a variety of excuses to get away from my clients, including another doctor's appointment, and telling them I need to meet with other clients. I can't say that I'm at the office, because if they call there, well, I can't ask anyone there to cover for me. I don't like this part of making up excuses for where I am; I'm sure I'll slip up sooner or later.

In looking for good lawyers, I tried everything, including the phone book, internet, and a friend of my wife's family. He's a lawyer, but not a business lawyer. He suggested one person, and I found the other two through my own research of local law firms. It helped that I've worked with some law firms over the years and also knew a little bit about their reputations, but just like with George and I, I'm sure you can get two people from the same firm with different approaches.

I've met with three business lawyers this week: One lawyer from a very large firm, one from a mid-sized firm, and one who owns his own small business. I didn't get a good feeling from the first lawyer at the large firm, it felt like I'd be a cog in a wheel there. I thought the person at the mid-size firm was very bright, but a little on the timid side. I liked the third lawyer, the one who owns his own business; he also seems bright, and very aggressive. The last two charge $150 per hour, while the first one wanted to charge $185/hour.

On the assumption that I'm going to have to deal with Jack a lot during this process, I'm going with the third business lawyer, Joe, the aggressive one. I have no problem in writing this here today: If I'm going to have to deal with Jack, I want someone that will be aggressive and make his life miserable. (You can see why I wouldn't have made it as a monk.)

As we talked, he also mentioned that I'll want to get to know a tax attorney, as they can save you a big pile of money during a business sale. He gave me the name of a tax attorney downtown, and said he was possibly the best in town. The tax attorney charges $200 per hour, but he told me he's very sharp, works fast, and it would be a great investment. He said, "In words of Adrian Monk, you'll thank me later."

I met again with Joe (my new business lawyer) late this afternoon. He said he wouldn't always be able to meet this rapidly, but he had a break in the schedule, and knew I was in a hurry. He read the pertinent parts of our business Operating Agreement, and said I needed to follow it to a tee. He's saying everything I already knew, but told me that since Jack was a wildcard, I needed to make it all very formal.

The first order of selling my shares was to make a formal, written offer to "the company." That is, I need to state in very clear terms what I want to sell my shares for, put it all in writing, and address it to the Company, which really means addressing it to the other Class A partners.

He reiterated what I already knew: The Company has thirty days to approve or revoke the offer, at which point I can make the same offer to the Class A partners, and they will also have thirty days to respond. Assuming they don't want to make a purchase, I can then go to the Class B partners with the same offer, giving them another thirty days. Only after going through this process can I make an offer to any outside entities.

If everyone in this process really takes thirty days to make a decision, we'll be into December before I can even think about talking to any outside entities. I told him I was sure that the Company wouldn't take the offer, as Jack owns the majority of the shares after me, and he's scared. If he really wants this matter to be settled he'll push the Company to reject my offer fast so I can get to the next steps.

Since Jack told me he won't approve for the company to buy my shares, I assume he won't make an offer to buy my shares as a Class A member either. While David might like to buy some of my shares, I don't think he can afford to buy them all, and I also don't think he'd *want* to buy them all.

One important point Joe made clear here was that I can't make David a different offer than I make to Jack. It was clear to Joe that I don't want to sell anything to Jack, but he stressed that I can't make a different deal to David right now.

So assuming that David won't buy all my shares, I next move on to the Class B members. I've already mentioned that Cooper would like more ownership in the company, so he should be good for a few percent, and George should also be very interested in the opportunity. I'm not sure about anyone else, and of course I'm not sure what anyone is really willing to pay.

Joe promised to work up his part of the paperwork by the end of the day Saturday. He said he normally works Saturday, and wouldn't charge overtime for it. But, he said, I needed to give him a solid sales price that I wanted.

One other important note here: I don't want Jack to profit from this in any way, but I would like to find a way to sell to David and the Class B partners. Joe suggested I set my asking price at $12K per share so the Company would reject it, followed by the Class A members rejecting it. I could then make the same offer to the Class B partners, they would reject it, and then I could negotiate with anyone I wanted.

He also said that based on what I had told him, I'd need to keep selling "comfort" to the Class B partners, who might be even more scared than Jack seemed by my leaving. We decided that in my discussion with them I should keep repeating these points:

- I'm not leaving until late next spring.
- I'll do whatever I can to help in the transition.
- David will pick up my projects.
- George will handle the "sales engineer" role.
- This is a great opportunity for everyone to increase their roles and ownership in the company, and make more money.

When our bookkeeper (my ex-wife) asked me today what a bill from the company attorney was for, I called him up. He told me he talked to Jack about an issue related to the sale of the company. I reminded him that he was supposed to be neutral in all of this, but he just gave Jack advice, without either one of them notifying me, and then sent a bill to the company.

After asking him to explain himself, I fired him, and told him that if he wanted to be reimbursed for his legal advice, he needed to send his bill to Jack, because I just shredded it.

I followed that with an email to Jack, telling him to expect the lawyer's bill, because the company would not pay for his personal legal advice, and cc'd David on the email. I also informed them that I had fired the attorney, and that the Class A partners -- including me -- needed to find a new attorney.

After thinking it over, I told Joe to go with the $12K per share approach, and he sent a legalized version of an offer letter back to me yesterday afternoon. I forwarded that letter to David and Jack in an email and asked if they could meet Monday evening to look at it. David replied "yes" yesterday, and Jack, who could have been dead for all I knew, also replied "yes" tonight.

MONDAY, SEPTEMBER 5, 2005

I made my sales offer to the Company (via the Class A partners) after hours today. I kept the offer at $12K per share, with the motivation being to make sure the Company rejected it.

I was correct in that assessment. I could barely get through all the details of the sales offer, including the $12K per share price, my offer to stay until April 30th of next year, a salary of $100K per year until I left, and a willingness to help in most transition matters, except for working with Jack. Just as I was saying there was one caveat to my offer, which was that I wanted to talk to my tax attorney this week about the actual buyout/payment terms, I was interrupted.

The good news here is that Jack seemed relatively calm, and just said flat-out that he wouldn't approve of this while acting in the capacity of the Company, so there was no point in discussing it. I asked David if he wanted to discuss this with Jack in private, and he said no.

I halfheartedly tried to talk them into the deal, telling them that we still needed to hire a company attorney, but that I thought after the purchase the remaining shares would be evenly split between the Class A partners (and possibly the Class B partners), and that was a good deal for everyone, with no money out of their pockets, here's how the payments might work, etc.

Before the meeting I really thought I'd need to leave the room, and that they might want to take a few days to think about this, but to my surprise, I never left the room, and the matter was resolved right then and there. I asked them to sign one copy of my offer on the line stating that as the remaining Class A partners they were rejecting the offer on behalf of the Company.

Normally we'd file something like this in the company folder in the locked file cabinet, but in this case the partners decided they didn't want this document in the office. So I made one copy for each of us, and we took them home with us.

Before the meeting ended I told them I would follow up with the same offer to them as Class A partners very soon. I told them I couldn't get it all done today, but I might do it tomorrow, but since I was scheduled to meet with my tax attorney on Wednesday, I would probably wait until then. I reminded them that at that point, they could make up their minds individually, with either or both of them accepting my offer to sell personally.

I also reminded them that as a company we had to find a new attorney. Normally this is something I would do myself, but David stepped in and suggested he should do this, perhaps with George and Cooper. He said George and Cooper would know about everything soon enough, and given the tension between Jack and I, perhaps they could try to find someone.

I asked them to come up with three alternatives they liked, and then we'd choose one from that pool. I didn't have to do this at all, but I was trying to keep some peace in the group. I gave David the names of the two attorneys I just hired and told him they were off limits, but they could check around with anyone else they wanted. I didn't give them the names of the other two attorneys I had talked to; I debated about this briefly, but I didn't want to influence them.

I met with Dan (the business tax attorney) today, and true to Joe's word, he's very sharp, and very quick. I didn't need to repeat anything, and he didn't babble on like our previous business attorney.

In my earlier discussions with Joe, he suggested trying to receive all my payments from the partners -- who I assumed would buy my shares eventually -- as regular cash payments, but Dan said no, given the situation, the best way to get paid was to have as much of the payments to me classified as "goodwill." While any other form of payment would be taxed as ordinary income -- and the first rule of a tax attorney is that ordinary income is bad -- goodwill payments would only be taxed at 15%.

As an example, to use round numbers, let's say I received $100K from the partners who wanted to buy my interest. If all of this is taxed as goodwill, my net would be $85K, but if it's taxed as ordinary income, in a tax bracket of 33% or higher, my net would be only $67K -- a very substantial $18K (18%) *minimum* difference.

Goodwill

Dan said I was eligible for this "personal goodwill" treatment for a variety of reasons. First, I was the founder of the business and the majority shareholder. Second, throughout the history of the company a large majority of the revenue of the business had come through me. Third, I have done a fair amount of public speaking. Putting these things together, he said it was very easy to argue that most people who thought of the company really thought of me. I'll confess that I don't know the exact definition of goodwill, but that's how I remember him explaining it to me.

There are a couple of technical issues here on how much of the sales price can be classified as goodwill, and how much can't, and I don't understand all of this yet. A second part to this is that I need to get the partners and the company accountant to buy off on this, but he said that this shouldn't be a huge problem. He reiterated that I couldn't get all 100% of the sales price classified this way, but again I don't understand all the accounting terms yet, and can't say exactly why this is.

We also talked about a variety of ways that I might be paid, including (a) getting all the cash up front, (b) getting some cash up front and some deferred, and (c) getting all the cash in a deferred manner, presumably from the cash flow of the business. He strongly advised getting all the cash up front, especially if I was leaving town. In fact, he said he would demand that approach if I asked him to represent me in any further way on this deal. He said he's seen so many long-term buyouts fail in so many different ways that he wouldn't be competent if he allowed me to go for a long term payout, and it would be well worth taking a little less money up front just to make sure I got paid close to what I wanted.

Besides those reasons, he said there would be a clause in the closing docs that Kentucky would be the state of jurisdiction for the sale, and if I was serious about going to Alaska, that would be a problem for me.

The whole meeting ended in 2.5 hours, and I was extremely happy with the results. I had just spent $500, but it seems like $500 with a potential payback in the five- or six-figure range, that's one heck of an investment.

I talked to Joe, and shared the information that Dan gave me. Joe joked about how it sure was a wonderful suggestion of his to talk to a tax attorney, wasn't it? I agreed with him that it was, and agreed with his assessment that Dan was as sharp as they come.

We talked about how to include this in my offer letter to the Class A partners, but Joe suggested not mentioning it at all. Now that we knew this, he said, let's keep it under our belts, and pull it out later, after we get some people to agree to buy my shares at a good price.

So we kept that line off the offer letter we were working on, and he said that if anyone asked what I talked to the tax attorney about, I should just say that he said, "it depends" a lot, and that he really didn't have any advice to offer at this time, and that I should come back to him when I had a firm offer.

Since David and Jack didn't seem to know other attorneys, and because Joe himself didn't know about the goodwill approach, it should be easy to get away with this. I won't say that I was about to lie, I just wasn't going to share everything I just paid almost $1,000 to two different attorneys to learn.

Selling a business is like playing poker

Really, this doesn't feel like lying nearly as much as it feels like poker -- very high stakes poker. If everything goes very wrong the company could explode and I'd be left with nothing, except maybe a big mess, with all the partners leaving to start a new company. (Having written that, I suddenly feel a strong need to look at our Operating Agreement again, as well as our Non-Competition Agreement.)

So I have to be careful. Unless David is willing to pay my asking price as a Class A partner (I won't really let him do that), I need to get them to reject my offer so I can get to the Class B partners, get them to reject the offer, and avoid upsetting everyone as much as possible during the process.

After work today -- after the close of business on a Friday evening -- I made the same offer to the Class A business partners as I made to them earlier this week when they were working on behalf of the Company. This time, however, I told them they were free to think about this individually, they didn't have to agree together, and either one could buy all of my shares individually.

I also told them that the only way I could legally talk to the Class B members was if they rejected this. So the decision was now theirs, if they wanted a shot at buying my shares without the Class B members involved, this was my offer, but if they didn't want to, the next step was to involve the Class B members, which I would do immediately after my offer was rejected.

I told them that since the company didn't have an attorney at the moment, all of this was free legal advice for the time being. I said I was very certain that it was correct, that we had been told all of this by our previous attorney, and I was following the advice of my personal attorney very strictly now.

Jack was generally silent in this meeting, only saying that he had no interest in buying anything. Between that and all of my other anger at him, I directed all of my discussions at David. Truth be told I wasn't trying to sell David too hard, because I didn't think he wanted to buy all the interest or could afford to at my current price, and I really didn't want to sell to him at this high price, I just had to go through the formality.

Since Jack had already said, "No" verbally, I asked him to sign the document I gave him, putting in writing that he rejected my offer as a Class A member. He wouldn't do that though. I asked him why, since he had already said no. He said he was tired, and didn't want to do it tonight.

David didn't say he was tired, but also said that he didn't want to sign the document tonight, that he wanted to think about it. I said that was fine, nothing had to be decided tonight, so we wrapped up our brief meeting. As I thought about it, I didn't want to leave Jack alone with David, so I made sure we all left together. If he was going to influence David, I wanted him to have to make a phone call, not stand out in the parking lot.

This really is a high-stakes game of poker, except I'm playing with my own money, and my own company.

Okay ... this process took a very unexpected turn today. David emailed me to see if we could meet somewhere, so we picked a lousy coffee shop that most people don't normally go to. When I got there David was joined by George and Cooper, our Class B partners.

I have no idea what the look on my face was when I saw them all, other than confusion. They apologized for ambushing me like this, but in short, Jack had already written David to say he wasn't interested in buying my shares, so David, assuming the next step for me being to talk to the Class B partners, made that arrangement for me, and in fact the three of them have been talking to each other since some time yesterday. David said that he told Jack about this last night, and Jack was fine with it.

After catching up to speed with all of that, and some jokes about this really being an intervention, I got a lousy cup of coffee, and the four of us began to talk. First, I told them that without Jack and David officially signing any paperwork, all we could talk about were "what if" scenarios. David said he would sign his paperwork after Jack signed his, and added that Jack had been "acting weird," so David wouldn't sign his until then. The three of them also told me this situation was causing them great personal stress, and the situation between Jack and I was making things worse.

History with a business partner

I thought about things for a little while, mostly going through the Operating Agreement in my mind, making sure that I could legally talk to them about my history with Jack. After I was satisfied that there was nothing illegal about what I was about to say about another partner, I told them how I had tried to buy his shares back two times at very reasonable rates, including my last $14K per share offer, the details of his interaction with our last attorney that resulted in me firing the attorney, and his "counter offer" to me at our aborted lunch.

I skipped some of my feelings about Jack that might make him seem like more of a liability; I still had to be in sales mode to some extent, and if they were happy with Jack as he was, so be it.

I told them that from my standpoint my relationship with Jack was over, and that if I was going to somehow stay with the company, he would have to go. However, because I wanted to leave the company and eventually return to my own hometown, I suggested they focus on Jack's strengths, and that if the three of them bought my shares they'd be in a strong position to deal with him. I told them I missed the old Jack, the one I started the company with. That was true, I did miss that person, but in my opinion, he wasn't around any more.

I told them that if the three of them were really interested in buying my shares, we needed to work through this legal process as fast as possible. The Class A partners needed to reject my offer, and then the Class B partners had to reject it, and after that I could talk to anyone I wanted to. I told them they'd have to trust me that I wasn't doing this just to talk to people outside the company, that what I really wanted to do was to sell to them, but this had to be a legal process, and my lawyer told me I had to take these steps.

I skipped telling them that I knew my asking price was too high. I still wanted Jack out of the picture, so I kept that to myself.

At the end of the meeting I asked them to trust me, and that after Jack and David turned me down, and then the Class B partners turned me down, I'd be glad to talk to them as a group again, but legally we had to go through those steps. Finally, I added that I wasn't going to change my mind, I really wanted to leave by next summer, and I thought this would be a "chance of a lifetime" opportunity for them to own their own business, a small business that was already established and successful.

I have to say, there was some serious stress involved, but I also feel like I'm also much closer to getting what I want, or at least what I think I want.

Jack officially rejected my offer to sell the company yesterday, followed by David. While I thought things were moving along on the fast track in a very positive way, this morning began with George suddenly threatening to quit.

He said all this stress was too much for him, that he could just quit the company, start consulting on his own, and make almost as much money as he could by being a business owner. He thought my asking price was unreasonable, and he felt like the company was about to explode.

My first thought was that Jack had put him up to this, but as I spoke to him I could see he was visibly upset, even trembling a little. I realized that maybe I had pushed him too hard. I've always thought consulting was stressful work, you're always meeting with new clients, working on new projects, and often learning new technologies on the fly, so I assumed the people that succeeded as consultants had more confidence in themselves, and could handle the stress. But for a guy who was so upset recently because he wanted more ownership in the company, he seems very, very scared right now.

When he mentioned going off to work on his own, I briefly thought about reminding him of our noncompete agreement, but if you know tech people at all, especially "open source" tech people, you know that would have been a disaster.

David was with George and I during this discussion, so to stall for time as much as anything, I asked David how he was feeling. He said he didn't want to do anything drastic, but yes, he agreed, this was extremely stressful, and wanted to see it end soon. He also said that he worked through the numbers himself, and thought my asking price was too high. He said a lot of bad things could happen after I left, and if they paid me up front (which was all we had talked about to date), I would win, and they would lose, and he needed something that was more of a win-win situation.

I was pleasantly surprised at his research and thought process, so between that and trying to get George to calm down, I decided to come clean and tell them more of the truth, things I had only hinted at on Sunday.

My selling price

I told them that because of the bad feelings between myself and Jack, the first thing I had to do was to officially get him out of the picture, and that part succeeded when he signed the rejection of my offer yesterday. I told them my asking price was intentionally too high because of two factors. First, I wanted to make sure Jack rejected it, both from a Company standpoint and then from a Class A standpoint. Second, it was my understanding that I legally had to keep the offer to the Class A partners the same as the offer to the Company, and I would also have to legally make the same offer to the Class B partners. Once everyone rejected the offer, my understanding was that we could begin discussions about what my shares were really worth.

I told them I agreed that my offer was too high, but I hoped they could see why I didn't say anything until now. (Shoot, I thought to myself, the Class B partners haven't even rejected my offer yet, and here I am telling them I know my asking price is too high. In most negotiations that would be a dumb tactic, but it seemed necessary here.)

I just asked them to trust me again, that if everyone will just reject my current offer I'll be glad to talk to whatever group of employees they want to put together to buy my shares -- as long as that group doesn't include Jack. I even put it in writing, scribbling a note on a sheet of paper saying that if the Class B members will reject my offer today or tomorrow, I'll be glad to meet with them immediately after that to talk turkey.

Again, I reiterated that I wanted them to own the company, though I avoided mentioning that I would take my offer to outside investors if I was forced to. Truth be told, I felt like it would take a long time to negotiate with anyone outside of the company, and the existing partners would have to agree to work with that outside entity, and all of that could be very difficult to make work.

By the end of the meeting George had calmed down, and was no longer threatening to sell his shares back to me. I again apologized for putting them through this, but I asked them to look at it from my standpoint, and know that I'm trying to keep everything legal as we go through this process. I also tried to get them to imagine a world where they owned the company by the end of October, after which I would be around until next summer to mentor them in any way I could.

New business attorney candidates

By the end of the meeting things had stabilized enough that they told me they really had only two candidates for a new company attorney, and they gave me their contact information. I told them I'd meet them this week if possible, and encouraged them to join me on the visits. If I had my way, I told them, this was going to be their company, and they might as well get used to these things, and they should be completely involved in this decision.

Finally, things had also stabilized enough that they suggested we all meet again Saturday morning to have the Class B partners reject my offer, and then discuss what my shares were really worth. We all had a lot of work to do this week, so nobody really wanted to meet during the week again, or even Friday night, when we'd all be tired.

They also suggested Saturday morning might be inconvenient for Jack, and he might skip it altogether, at which point I laughed. "Don't let me corrupt you on Jack," I told them, "other than the part where I won't sell my shares to him. You're going to have to work together in the future, unless you already have some plan you're not telling me. In either case, just insist on hiring a great salesperson, and you'll be fine."

David, George, and I met with the two business lawyers they suggested, and we choose the second one, a woman named Pam who worked at a midsize law firm. Like the other good lawyers I had come to know recently, she spoke directly, and without any extra legal-ease. She would have preferred to meet Jack as well, she said, but she's seen situations like this before, and understood. David and George chipped in that they had Jack's promise that he would go along with whatever we decided, which was interesting to hear. Although I try not to think about Jack, this was a reminder that he's still back there talking to the partners.

Like our first company attorney, she explained what she could and could not do in the process of selling the business, or at least in the process of me selling my interest in the business. She could help with everyday business legal matters, and could also write up the final business sales documents once I had agreed to sell my interest to someone else, presumably a group of partners. She could not help any of us individually, however, and suggested that I have my own attorneys, and the buying partners have their own attorneys.

We didn't tell her immediately that we had selected her, but it was obvious that the three of us liked her, and we made that decision in the parking lot. I called her on the way home to let her know of our decision, explaining that we all felt comfortable with her, and time was of the essence.

It was good to see David and George involved in this process; it's a little like watching them grow up. I wish Cooper could have been here as well, but he's a bit too busy at the moment, and he also doesn't seem too interested in legal matters like this.

As the last few days progressed, we all realized we'd be in no shape to have a serious discussion about selling my shares to the partners by Saturday. Some emergency issues came up at work, and we were all tired, but David, George, and Cooper still decided that we should meet for about ninety minutes.

We met at the office at 10 a.m., and we quickly got to the purpose of the meeting. With Jack out of the picture, at least for now, the Class B partners had a lot of questions they wanted to ask before officially rejecting my offer, including:

- What is the health of the company? ("Do you know something we don't know?")
- Why was the offer rejected by the Company and Class A partners?
- Can one of us buy your shares, or do we all have to buy?
- If we don't buy, do you have people lined up to buy outside of the company?
- Who will take over all the roles I currently play?

The most interesting question I hadn't even considered was, "Why don't I just open a new office of our company in my hometown?" For a brief moment I was intrigued by that idea, but at this point I really am set on taking a long vacation, and that was just a passing thought. Also, that idea didn't resolve the problem that Jack was still working at my company. If I opened a new office, I would still want him removed from the company.

While those were my thoughts, I told them that besides my desire to move, I was also burned out, and didn't know if I even wanted to continue in this industry any more. I told them I was working on various vacation plans for next year, and that's why I wanted to leave by early summer.

The second most interesting question was, "Why did the Company and Class A partners rejected my offer?" I told them I assumed they thought it was too expensive, and I turned the question over to David. I thought about asking them if they wanted me to leave the room while he answered that question, but I assumed they had really talked about this already, and I also didn't think it was really a big deal, especially after I told David and George that I knew my offer was priced too high.

David said that Jack just wouldn't go along with either approach, and that without Jack's vote, the Company definitely couldn't make an offer, and by himself he didn't have enough money to buy my interest. He also added that the share price was too high for him.

The partners open up

At this point everyone seemed to magically open up, and they started to share their real concerns. They were concerned about income from current business falling off when I left, and concerned about future sales with me gone. They also assumed that my former wife would leave the company when I left, so they'd need a new bookkeeper, and also thought several salaries would have to be adjusted. I was pleased with their analysis, if not their assumptions. They had clearly put some time into it, and it was thorough.

There really wasn't much for me to do, I just let everyone talk, only chiming in at one point to say that we have been told by several parties during the sales process that buyers typically look at breaking even somewhere down the road between two to five years, and that Jack himself had been set on three years. I also added that if the sale happened today, I'd still be with the company for somewhere between seven and nine months.

After everyone aired what they were thinking, I made an effort to resolve some of their concerns. I said David was in excellent shape to replace me at several accounts, that George was an excellent "Sales Engineer" (my term for a technical sales support person), and everyone else in the room now had at least five years experience in doing what we do as consultants, so there probably wasn't much else for me to teach them. Finally, I said, this is an opportunity for everyone to step up, an opportunity I was sure several of them were looking for.

I also told them I knew we were talking about a lot of money, but if they looked at what each of them had paid for their shares, and how much income they made from those shares over the years, they had to know that buying them was one of the best deals they'd made in their lives. If one or two individuals from the group couldn't afford to buy my shares by themselves, hopefully a larger group of them could.

Another great question came up during our discussion: Could the Class B partners have their shares converted to Class A shares during the purchase process? I have to admit, this was something I hadn't even thought about. Yes, I told them, that was possible, but the current Class A members would have to sign off on that. If I stayed with the company I could do that, but because I wanted to leave, and because they would get these shares as part of the sales process, this was probably something that David and Jack would have to agree to as part of the sales process.

That was the last major question I can recall. After that there was some idle chit-chat, with the partners asking "Are you sure?", and saying things like they would miss me, they were sorry about my divorce, and asked about my vacation plans. One partner asked if the reason I was in a bad mood one particular day recently had anything to do with this, and I laughed and said yes, it did. I told them this has been stressful on all of us, and I apologized for that.

As I mentioned earlier, we all had other commitments after a long work week, so we didn't have any time to talk about a real asking price.

The Class B partners had several more questions for me, which we handled by email. Their questions were straightforward, and mostly had to do with the numbers I was looking for.

They also asked for a guarantee that if the Class B partners rejected my offer, that I would come back to David and the Class B partners to negotiate a deal before going to an outside party. I told them that was absolutely fine by me, and that was my intent.

After answering their questions, the Class B partners told me they'd sign the documents to formally reject my offer, and asked if we could have a meeting to both (a) sign those papers and then (b) begin meeting to negotiate what I wanted for my shares. I said that was fine by me, but unfortunately, due to everyone's schedule, we can't meet until Saturday. We actually could meet Friday night, but based on our last Friday night meeting, we decided not to do that any more.

I have to say, I'm disappointed that they don't seem to trust me, that they won't sign the papers to reject my offer unless they're positive I won't go talk to someone else right away. Yes, I have mentioned that there are people outside the company that I might be able to sell my interest to, but I haven't pushed that point at all, and I've told them many times now that (a) I want to sell my shares to them, and (b) yes, I guarantee you that I will talk to you first. I'm trying to look at it from their standpoint, and I guess they feel vulnerable, but I keep looking at it from my standpoint, and I'm still the same guy they've all trusted for at least five years now, the same guy that kept them all employed during our worst business times in 2001 and 2002.

Besides those feelings, I was also curious, would Jack be at this next meeting?

Thursday, September 22, 2005

I have no idea what I've been thinking, but it really hit me this afternoon that I need to be prepared for some serious negotiating this weekend. Will the guys come to me with a serious counteroffer? Or will they just be looking to me for a more "reasonable" offer?

I was planning on going out with some friends tonight, but after thinking about this, I told them I'd have to take a raincheck. As I write these notes this evening, I'm making a fresh pot of coffee, and getting ready to work on some sales numbers I can live with, numbers that I also hope the partners will be able to go along with.

I was glad to see the people I wanted to see at the meeting this morning: All of the Class A and B partners, except for Jack. The meeting began with the Class B partners signing the documents to reject my offer to sell, and making copies of those documents for everyone.

After that, I was glad to see that the partners had tried to put an offer together for me, I appreciated their initiative. What I didn't appreciate was their offer.

Somewhere in their research they got the idea that the company was worth little more than "book value." Geez, now where could they have gotten that friggin' idea?

I was pissed that this was where we were going to start, pissed about where I thought they got this idea from, and also upset that they seemed very attached to this idea. I could tell this meeting wasn't going to go very well, and suddenly I was thinking what they didn't want me to think: Who could I sell my interest to outside of the company? My lawyer, Joe, seriously said he would be interested. Then there was Steve, Jerry, our major competitors ...

Discussing their "book value" offer

I sure didn't expect to have to start with a low-ball offer like this, and I had to put it down in a big hurry. I know these guys, and I know they didn't know much about business financials, so I felt like it was suddenly time for a training lesson.

As I've written here before, I explained to them that book value is really "fire sale value," and there isn't a fire right now. Fire sale value is when we decide to close the doors and go out of business, and we take what money we have in the bank, and we make a run for it. Or, you can argue that it would be the value of the company if I said, "Hey, guys, I've got the car engine running out in the parking lot, here's the keys to the building, good luck."

I reiterated to them that those situations weren't what we're looking at here. I've told you what my travel plans are, and I can guarantee you that this is not the time of the year to hop on a motorcycle and ride up to Alaska, not unless they make snow tires for motorcycles. I don't know how else I can say it, but I guarantee you I will be here until at least the end of April.

I explained book value to everyone in the room in great detail, and printed off a high-level (summarized) version of our current P&L statement and Balance Sheet. I showed them what the current book value was, and then I showed them what it would look like if we decided to take a distribution. (This wasn't a big deal, all of our partners can look at a summarized version of these reports at any time.)

In summary, I said it one last time: Book value is fire sale value, there are no fires here, I'm not leaving, and this isn't a reasonable offer now. If we can't come to an agreement until next spring, okay, that's when we can talk about a fire sale, but not now.

For the majority of the meeting I felt like I was back to square one with these guys, and while I was frustrated, I tried not to let it show, and instead tried to use it as an opportunity to train these guys a little more. But after this long discussion we were quickly running out of time. Some of the partners had other obligations, and we were going to have to reconvene another time.

I reiterated to the partners I was willing to negotiate and come down from my previous asking price, as promised, but book value was unreasonable. They would be "in the black" on the deal immediately, and that was no value to me at all.

As I thought about the phrase, "terms of an agreement," I suddenly realized how far we were from *any* agreement. We weren't even in the same ballpark on price, they didn't agree that I should get all the cash up front, and I hadn't yet told them about the goodwill part of the deal. We have a very long way to go.

I left the meeting with the realization that if I wanted this sale to happen any time soon, I was going to have to take the bull by the horns, do a whole bunch of work to come up with my own numbers, and justify those numbers to them. I'd have to show what I wanted, and clearly show how they were going to get paid back.

One other thing we all learned: Several partners have vacations coming up in the next few weeks, myself included, and those are going to slow down the sales process. I'm debating about skipping my own vacation, but it's already paid for, and overlaps with two of the partner's vacations, so at the moment I'm still planning to take it.

It took a while to get my own thinking where I wanted it to be, but I've finally finished creating what I call my "business value" spreadsheets.

After really digging into the problem and trying to think about what really makes sense, I finally decided to base everything on Marty's cash flow analysis approach, and look for a complete ROI for the business buyers in two years. I thought these terms were reasonable, but maybe just a little on the high side. I've mentioned that I personally would want an 18-month ROI, but I don't want to start that low. This is, after all, a negotiation.

Cash flow basis assumptions

While the decision to base my work on a cash flow basis sounds easy, I had to factor many things into my equations, including:

- I was leaving the business.
- My wife works full-time now, and she would also be leaving. Replacing her skills with at least one more full-time employee would be a little more expensive. (A combination bookkeeper, receptionist, and office manager isn't that easy to find.)
- I assumed David and George would split my duties, and the company would need to hire another good tech person at roughly $90K per year.
- All the Class B business partners would be converted to Class A partners. There was no obvious financial impact here, but their salaries are currently all over the board, and one impression I got was that they all wanted to take more or less the same salary. Therefore, I assumed they would all take salaries of $75K/year. Truthfully I expected them to want more than that, but again, this is my spreadsheet. They can change it however they want to after I give it to them. (The issue here is that if everyone takes a lower salary, Net Income will appear to be higher, partners with a higher percent ownership will get a higher ratio of that income. Conversely, if everyone takes a salary of

$100K/year, net income will be significantly lower, and owning my shares in the company will be less valuable. Again, not my problem.)

I expected Jack would also throw a wrench into this "equal partner salaries" concept, and might use this situation to try to negotiate a higher salary for his wife, but (a) I wasn't going to plant those seeds in anyone's mind, and (b) I just had to assume ideal conditions.

There were other factors to consider, but those were the most important.

Partner cash flows and earnings

It's a little strange contemplating my own business without me in it, it's a little like writing your own obituary after you're dead. But I worked through the spreadsheets until I thought everything felt right, and then I calculated the new cash flows back to the partners, assuming the business revenue stayed even. To me, there's no logical reason to assume that business revenue will go down rather than up. Again, David replaces me technically; we hire someone to back-fill his work; George takes on more sales engineer duties; we're not really out there selling anything right now, we're just maintaining current accounts; and I'm still here for 7-9 months; not a big deal.

One thing the partners have made clear several times now is that they want me to be paid out through the earnings of the company, and while I can see their logic -- my payout should at least be partially based on whether the company fails or succeeds after I sell -- the lawyers advice to get all the cash up front is still in my mind. The other part of this I don't like is that if they can't keep the projects running smoothly without me, or if Jack can't sell things, those aren't my problems.

That being said, I worked up a spreadsheet where I get 75% of the money up front, and 25% of the money in payouts during the first 12 months of the deal. They probably want something more like a 50/50 split over 18-24 months, but I won't agree to that.

Partner tax consequences

During this process I also realized a flaw in Marty's logic that was very depressing -- the tax consequences to the partners.

For example, let's say we worked through all the numbers, and we determined that my shares were worth $500K (to use a simple, even number). By my calculations, this meant that the net income that would be distributed to the remaining partners should equal $500K on the 24th month of the deal, assuming they agreed to a 24-month ROI.

The problem with this deal -- I suddenly realized -- was that all the money going to them was taxable. So even if $500K in net income flowed to them from the shares they bought from me, that $500K would be taxed at a rate of 33% or more. This was a huge blow to my calculations. If this was right, it would take them 33% longer to really recoup their investment. Am I thinking about this right?

Ugh. After looking at this for some time I've finally decided that I need to talk to my tax attorney again.

David and George have become the voice of the new partner coalition, and they asked me today when I'll be ready to meet again. I told them I was working on some spreadsheets, but ran into a delay yesterday, and I also wanted to talk to my attorney about some of the particulars. I told them I hoped to get back with them on Wednesday, but I wasn't sure if I could meet with my lawyer by then. I didn't mention that I was going to be talking to my *tax* attorney, because I don't want them to start thinking about tax consequences unless it's necessary, and it's still possible that I'm wrong here. I don't want to screw them, but I also don't want to scare them.

More tax attorney discussions

I put in a call to my tax attorney (Dan), and by the end of the day we had a chance to talk. I explained my spreadsheet to him, how I was looking at a cash flow analysis, etc., and he said I was right, but I really needed to look at it as though an outside corporation was buying my shares.

If an outside corporation bought my shares, that corporation would receive the net income from my business as an income to their business, just like any other form of revenue. Their business could then take all sorts of deductions against that income (car leases, golf course memberships, etc.), so they wouldn't be paying taxes on that net income directly. They could take that example $500K in income, take all their deductions, and then pay taxes on some significantly smaller amount. Shoot, he said, in an extreme situation, their business could even have an overall loss, and in that case they wouldn't have to pay any taxes on the $500K net income that flowed to their business.

He explained that there are many variations on this, but that I shouldn't worry about the tax consequences here. He said that if a 24-month ROI was what we were looking at, I should ignore the tax consequences, and just work it out so the new cash flows to the partners (salary and distributions) would get them their $500K back in 24 months. Because he's my attorney he said he couldn't work with them on this, but that they should consult their own tax attorney to learn how to best handle this.

He also reminded me of the value of *thinking in extremes*. He told me that since I was making up the spreadsheets, I could make the salaries of all the partners $1/year. Assuming there were five partners, and we reduced their base salaries from $80K/year to $1/year, this would increase the company's net income by $400K/year. He said that wasn't necessarily a normal approach, but since I was creating the spreadsheets, I could do whatever I wanted. He also reminded me that this is why I can never agree to be paid out of the company's net income after I leave; net income can be made to appear very large, or nonexistent, depending on the partner's salaries and other expenses.

I thanked Dan again for his time, and I also appreciated that he understood what I was talking about almost immediately. I thought this might take a while to explain, but he knew immediately what I was talking about.

While I understood everything he said, I knew that if I were in the partner's shoes, I'd want the cash that I took out of my bank account to buy the company to be completely replaced in twenty-four months, tax considerations included.

I'm still going to think about this for a while, but my current plan is to follow Dan's advice, and present my spreadsheet without this tax information, but I'm sure the partners will figure this out, and there will be some sort of negotiation. I thought about reducing all their salaries to $1 in my spreadsheets, but I see a lot of problems in going down that road, so I'm going to stay with my current assumption that they'll all take equal $75K salaries.

With a flurry of email, the partners and I arranged to meet tonight at the office. With the vacations starting to affect our schedule on Saturday, we all thought it was best to try to squeeze in a meeting.

I asked if they had come up with anything different since our last meeting, and they said no, they thought the ball was in my court, and they wanted to see what I came up with. I said that was true, and that I'd put a *lot* of time into this, and began to explain what I had.

Explaining my spreadsheets

Playing the role of a person selling his business, I first asked, "Do you think it would be reasonable for you to get a 100% return on your investment in 24 months? That is, if the sale happened today, I'd stay here about eight months, and then 16 months after that you'd have all your money back? Do you think that's reasonable?"

Unfortunately they didn't all say, "Yes" as I hoped, and generally just said, "It depends." With that, I began explaining everything I could about my cash flow analysis: How we agreed many months ago that twenty-four months seemed like a very viable buyout period, and all the other factors I had put into the spreadsheets, including all the partners taking a common salary.

By the end of the meeting I could tell that they still thought my asking price was too high, but they didn't have any logical reason for saying that. They thought my numbers looked real, and I wasn't playing games, but they also argued that the company revenue would surely go down. I asked why they thought that, and tried to get them to explain their reasoning, and reiterated that they already knew what I knew, now they just had to go out there and do it, and in regard to the sales process, George had already been doing it for quite some time now.

Unfortunately the meeting wasn't the great success I hoped it would be. Despite all my work, research, and some sales effort, it felt very uneven, and the partners seemed very stressed again. They seem unhappy with my offer, and unhappy that these vacations are coming up. Other than ignoring the tax implications, I feel like I've done a lot of work for them, tried to accelerate the schedule, and make this is as easy as possible for them, so this was a real disappointment.

At the end of the meeting I brought up the upcoming vacations, and asked everyone what they thought we should do, and they said we should all keep our current plans. I told them that even though I was going out west again, they could contact me at any time, and as long as I had phone or internet access, I'd be glad to try to work things out with them.

Book value thoughts

The meeting ended with no promises. It's obvious that my asking price is still too high for them, and if Jack gave them the idea of book value, he's done them a big disservice. There's a huge difference between book value and what I just laid out for them, and while everything I put together (except for the tax consequences) seems reasonable to me, once you've been told you can get something for a bargain basement price, I'm sure it's going to take a while to realize that a much higher price is actually reasonable. I wasn't really expecting a "Yes, we'll take it" response today, but I was hoping this would be the start of a healthy negotiation.

In other news, the partners won't tell me how they plan to split up my shares, assuming we ever get a deal done. They told me that they're trying to work that out between themselves, and the only thing I really needed to know was that they intended to buy it all, so I wouldn't have to look for outside buyers. They didn't say this in a mean-spirited way, just in a matter-of-fact way.

I agreed to send them my spreadsheets by email, but we didn't agree on a date to meet next. It sounded like George and David might tentatively represent the group while all the vacations were happening, but David was scheduled for a few days off himself, so it's not clear when we'll meet again. That, and it's obvious they're going to need some time to digest this, and see that I'm mostly right.

MONDAY, OCTOBER 3, 2005

A friend of mine was killed in a plane crash last week, and I went to his wake and funeral this weekend. I met him through a business deal many years ago, and as I spoke to some people at the funeral, I realized I've owned the company for ten years now, and in that ten years, there have been ten deaths between my family and friends.

I wasn't extremely close to this person, but that was mostly because we lived seventy miles apart. Although we met through business, it was one of those relationships where you immediately feel very close to someone, even though you're essentially strangers. I taught a Unix/Linux class for his company, and he participated in the class, and we laughed so hard it never felt like work. After that we sent emails back and forth, mostly jokes, worked a few customer projects together, and shared a few meals when we were in the same town together. We both joke around a lot, but when it comes to taking care of a customer, I know from experience we had the same feelings.

One of my favorite memories of working with him involved going to his office one Friday morning. He owned the business with two of his brothers, and they were all late for a meeting we had scheduled. While waiting, I went into the kitchen of their office to make some coffee, and when I opened the garbage can lid to throw out the old coffee grounds, I saw several empty bottles of liquor, and realized why they were all late. I took the empty bottles out of the garbage can, put them on the floor in the conference room next to my chair, and went back to making the coffee. When they finally showed up, they apologized, explaining they had a meeting late last night. I picked the bottles up off the floor, placed them on the conference room table, and asked if these were part of their meeting. We all laughed pretty hard, and they said they got a little overzealous celebrating a deal they had just won. This interaction was typical of most of our encounters.

Not much else you can say. The world just lost a really good guy.

I met with George and David at a coffee shop this afternoon to answer their questions related to my spreadsheets. The technical questions they asked were interesting, but the positioning between George and David was more interesting to me. I've noticed George taking more of an active leadership role in these meetings lately, especially today, while David seems to be regressing a little bit, back into his "I just want a job" personality.

Regarding my spreadsheets, they're still reworking my numbers, but they think I'm *way* too high. They seem to have figured out the "tax consequences" problem, so they're trying to figure out how to adjust for that. The obvious answer is that they should immediately reduce my figure by 33%, but they don't seem to want to just come out and say that.

I told them that from my perspective I can't think that way, because an outside entity won't think like that. I explained that I talked to my tax attorney, and I explained how an outside would look at this purchase, how they could deduct all their expenses, etc. I told them my tax attorney can't help them, they should talk to a tax attorney of their own about how to handle this. All of that being said, I assume we'll end up negotiating this, and I'd be fine if we just split this down the middle at 16.5%.

Payout from business revenue

They also want a 50/50 split on how I'm paid out, with 50% cash up front, and the other 50% coming from the revenue of the business, basically an *earn-out*. (At first they wanted to base it on the net income of the business, and I told them there was no way I was going there, and explained all the badness about that.) They think a 50/50 payout is a much more fair way to deal with the risk of losing business after I leave.

They're also worried about me leaving and then competing with them, but I countered that concern with two arguments. First, I'm planning on a long vacation and then returning to my hometown. Second, why would I start a new company? I'd just take Jack up on his offer to sell his interest, and stay with my company.

I didn't argue about the 50/50 earn-out idea today. I don't want to get into something like that without having any idea what they're really willing to offer.

They also said they didn't necessarily agree with the 24-month ROI plan, and that my offer didn't account for me not staying very long after the sale. Based on what they're heard all along, they thought that if I sold the company to an outside entity I would have to stay 12-18 months after the sale, and here I was, looking to leave town in 7-9 months, and we aren't anywhere near a deal yet.

As a final note, they also said they want to find a lawyer to represent their group, and haven't done that yet. I expect that's going to take at least another week, unless they found some they liked when they were searching for a company attorney.

I thought they would bring my numbers down some, but they're bringing them down even more than I expected. In positive news though, they seem happy, and nobody is talking about quitting.

Back in the regular business world, all of our projects are rolling along very well right now, though I'm concerned that all of these extra phone calls and meetings are causing missed time for all of us. If any of our other employees are talking to each other, they'll soon realize that the partners are having a lot of meetings with each other. However, I can't think of any other way to handle this, other than to communicate more by email, and postpone our phone conversations until after hours.

I called my lawyer today to talk about a couple of things related to the business sale, and specifically mentioned that the partners wanted to pay me 50% up front and 50% as an earn-out. He repeated what he and Dan had both said earlier, that I should absolutely not take that offer. He didn't give me any specific examples I can remember right now, but he said there are too many ways for people to wiggle out of deals like that, and all the money should come up front.

He also said that while they were stating it as the business partners trying to minimize their risk, he said I needed to look at it as opening up myself to the risk of their potential incompetence, infighting, possible turnover, etc. I told them none of them were incompetent, but that certainly with all the partner shares moving around, there could be some infighting. The possibility for turnover is also there, and indeed, Jack may negotiate his own deal as soon as I leave. While I've written about a lot of concerns I have with Jack, at least he offers them some stability in the sales area. At the very least he's capable of picking up the phone and talking to customers, where most of the technical people seem to avoid that as much as possible.

The truth about the 50/50 split regarding upfront cash and an earn-out is that I won't go there, and George knows it, or should know it. Before I started this company, I worked at another consulting firm in town. After I left that company, they bought another company here in town, promised to pay those owners their money in four equal payments, then went bankrupt after the first payment. This meant the people who sold to them not only lost their business, they also got only 25% of what they expected.

The reason I say George should know this is that he had some distant relatives involved in this transaction, and we talked about it many years ago.

A great piece of advice from my lawyer

When I told Joe that my partners were trying to build all the negative possibilities into their offer to make it as low as possible, he told me one thing that made a ton of sense. He said that as long as nobody was threatening to quit any time soon, a very good tactic is simply to delay the sale. In short, between salary and distributions, I make almost $1K/day for every day I own the company with the current ownership shares, so the longer we don't come to an agreement, the more money goes into my pocket. Put another way, if I can get the same offer from the partners in December that they're willing to make now, I'll leave in the summer with at least $90K more in my pockets if I don't accept their offer until then.

He didn't offer any specifics on how to "stall," but just said that if I didn't like what they were offering, I was under no obligation to sell, especially if everything was peaceful.

He added his advice that he's seen most sales end up horribly, but those that were "successful" ended up in one of two ways: Either everybody is happy (win/win), or nobody is happy (lose/lose). In any other arrangement, one group ends up happy and the other group isn't (win/lose), so he suggested I needed to keep pushing for what I wanted until the other partners couldn't take it any more. He said yes, this is risky, but at least I'd know that I was getting all I could get.

After I hung up with him, I was reminded that it feels weird to do battle against a group of people I personally hired. I hired them, trained them, invested in them, and now as I try to sell my business ownership to them, we're on opposite ends of the table, and I have to use everything I know about them to try to get what I want before I leave.

Everything has been quiet with the partners, other than getting a note from them saying they have a meeting scheduled with a business attorney this week. I reminded them that my vacation is coming up next weekend, so if they could do anything this week I'd be glad to look at it.

With nothing to do this weekend, I first went to see a movie, then came back to my apartment and began packing and organizing my things. I normally don't let myself think about something as distant as packing and leaving, especially when there's so much yet to be done, but today it felt great to just say, "Screw it," and to not think about work or this sales process, and just enjoy the thoughts of leaving and taking that long vacation.

WEDNESDAY, OCTOBER 12, 2005

George and David have made remarkably little progress on their business offer since our last meeting. They won't be seeing their lawyer until tomorrow, but since I'm leaving on vacation Friday night they wanted to see if I could meet late this afternoon. I agreed, not knowing why they wanted to meet.

When we met they asked if I had a chance to review their last numbers, like the ball was somehow in my court. Not sure where they were going with this, I told them yes, I had looked at them, but (a) I already told them I thought my offer was reasonable, (b) we discussed that they needed to talk to a tax lawyer, and (c) I was under the impression they were going to take their work to their new lawyer and discuss everything with him.

They seemed a little upset, so I kept asking if there was something I was supposed to have done. If I have any strength in meetings at all, it's usually in summarizing the meeting at the end and then assigning action items, and it was very clear to me that there was nothing for me to do after our last meeting.

When I thought I had made that clear -- and they didn't object with me -- they again asked what I thought of their last numbers. I told them again I didn't agree with a lot of it. I reiterated that I couldn't think about the tax consequences of them buying the company, because (a) Marty never included that in his calculations, (b) my lawyers had told me it was perfectly correct for me not to think of those, and (c) if negotiations with them broke down, I'd have to sell my shares to an outside entity, and this tax discussion wouldn't be an issue. Once again, I told them they needed to talk to a lawyer about how to handle this from their end.

I also rebutted their other reasons for trying to give me a lowball number, but I finally said, "Listen, you need to talk to your business attorney before we really talk about this any more. I'm sure they'll have more to add, and there's no use in us getting into all of this right now."

I have no idea where they're coming from right now, but they've gone back to being very nervous all over again.

Taking a break from all things business, I flew out to southern California last night to start my vacation. I'm just going to enjoy staying at different places along the coast, and eventually hook up with some old friends who moved here after college.

I told the partners they could reach me by phone most days, but there would be a couple of days I wouldn't be able to reply for sure. They aren't happy with me for taking this vacation, but I reminded them that they said it was okay a few weeks ago, and if they really wanted me to not take my vacation, they were going to have to reimburse me for my expenses. I don't like to play hardball like that, but I didn't think it was right for them to suddenly be upset about this. I reminded them that I didn't complain about their vacations.

They're definitely upset and nervous about something, but I don't know what it is. I hope they're just frustrated by the delay of meeting with their new lawyer.

The crazy thing is that with these delays, I'm reminded of my lawyer's advice to stall. Even as I sit out here in sunny California doing nothing on this beautiful afternoon, I'm making about $1K/day. Maybe the partners have figured this out, and that's why they're upset? Still, they need to make me a firm offer, and they haven't even done that yet.

As I think about their nervousness -- and their impending lowball offer -- I'm also thinking that I need to start talking to some outside people to gauge their interest (or non-interest) in buying my shares. At the moment I don't have a backup plan, and I always have a backup plan.

I'm not in a great mood today, and as part of that, I realized that I do currently have a backup plan, one I hadn't thought of. If we can't come to terms, I'll just drag this out as far as possible, maybe even until next spring, then take whatever offer I can get from them, or ... shut down the business, and take whatever money out of the bank is legally mine at that time.

Of course I don't want to that, but in this state of mind, that crossed my mind. While they can't seem to take the stress, I can stretch this out to the spring if I need to.

The business partners sent me their spreadsheets, which are basically unchanged, and asked me to negotiate against them, telling them specifically what I want in each area. Not to be a dick about it, but I feel like I already told them that in my previous spreadsheets. What else is there to say?

I delayed for a while in replying to them, and told them internet access in the current area is hit and miss, plus by just getting this to me now they're also hitting a time where I have planned events with my friends out here, but I'll do what I can.

Oh, and they're also unwilling to share anything their business attorney has told them, so this "sharing" I've been doing with them is a one-way street. But I guess that's to be expected, I'm trying to sell them something, so I have to do what I have to do to make the sale, while they don't have to share anything. Our friendships are very much taking a break right now.

I was hoping for a formal offer from them or their lawyer, but this is all I got. We could have done this ten days ago. And here I thought I was supposed to be the one stalling.

The short story for today is that I told the partners it just wasn't working out for me to review their spreadsheets after I received them Thursday, that I just had too many events planned with my friends. I told them I'd do what I could while traveling, and I did look at their spreadsheets a little more today.

After reviewing their spreadsheets, I drafted an email with these points:

- I can't agree to a 33% discount for their tax concerns, but since I'm willing to sell to them (the business partners) for less than an outsider, I'd gladly compromise and reduce that part of the formula to 16.5%, splitting the difference with them.

- They also wanted to reduce the 24-month ROI to 18 months. I told them I didn't agree with that, so I deleted their discount here. (It may end up at 21 months, but I'm not giving up on that one easily, especially not in combination with the first discount.)

- I told them I didn't agree with their argument for me staying around 12-18 months. That is something you'd do for an outside entity coming into the company brand new, someone that needs to learn how things are done and meet the customers, and I've worked with all of them for five or more years, and that's not necessary. They already know much more about me and our business than an outsider would ever know. So I deleted their discount for this line item.

- My lawyers are very opposed to me accepting payments over time, and I would need to talk to them about this. (This was admittedly a stalling tactic on my part.)

Business negotiating

I was always taught that in sales negotiating, you should never give up something without getting something else in return. We've always done this with our customers in sales meetings, and I have to say, it works; whenever a customer wants a discount, we always ask for something in return, and we've always gotten it. So by agreeing to split the 33% tax issue with them, I decided to add some things of personal value to me at the office that I wanted.

There is some furniture I put into the company in the early days, and I want it back. I could probably just take it, but I want it to be clear and legal. I also want to be able to keep the two work computers I use regularly, as well as some networking equipment and my office furniture at home. None of this would affect them, I told them, but they would need to get Jack's approval. Since all of these items have a low worth I didn't expect it to be a problem, but I wanted to have them, and the lawyers said to make sure everything is in writing.

As usual, I haven't told them about the "goodwill" part of the agreement. I'm going to make sure I get the best deal I can before adding that item to the sales agreement. I've done this sort of thing with car dealers before. I'm normally extremely direct with dealers when buying a new car ("Here's what I want, here's what I'm willing to pay"), but I also hold a couple of extra requests back until the last moment, and that's what I'm planning to do with the goodwill clause.

Sending this email out on a Sunday seems precarious. If they don't like my counteroffer for some reason, we're going to start the week off in a really bad mood. But if I don't send it to them, they're also going to be upset. Hopefully the 16.5% compromise will be a good start, and they can come back with the 21-month suggestion.

I'm not sure how else to say this, other than wow, the "partner coalition" is pissed.

While I thought we were still negotiating, they've come across in emails over the last twenty-four hours like the spreadsheet they sent me was their best offer, take it or leave it, and they are furious. Nobody has threatened to quit again, but they've told me we are way off, and that I'm "not negotiating in good faith."

I told them they said I should make the changes to their spreadsheets I thought were appropriate, and that's what I did. They certainly didn't mention anything about this being their "best offer" when they sent them.

Frankly, I'm pissed off too, because I don't think they're being reasonable. They don't want to compromise on anything. I really expected them to come back agreeing with the compromise on the tax situation and something like a 21-month ROI, and then I'd work with my lawyers, tell them about the goodwill clause, and then the paperwork would take as long as it needed to take.

Now I don't know where we are. We just have one person out on vacation now, but George and David are still playing the lead for their group, and we've agreed to meet Thursday morning for breakfast. I told them to invite any partner that wanted to come, but they've indicated it will just be them. I didn't push them too hard, because they're already upset, but I did ask them to look at things from my perspective.

If I wasn't dealing with geeks I'd think they were doing all of this as a negotiating tactic, but I can only guess that they think they're offer is reasonable. When I do the math, their offer doesn't work out to be much more than book value, and that's just not reasonable right now. This makes me think that Jack is coaching them, but I have no way of knowing that.

Breakfast this morning started off like I was sitting across the table from two angry people I barely knew. I've met with customers on troubled projects who were much less upset than these guys, and these guys were supposed to be my business partners. My first thoughts were that we shouldn't have done this in a public place.

I let them talk for a while, and then tried to reassure them that I'm still the same guy they've worked with for over five years. I've taught them everything I know, I've tried to mentor them, teach them about consulting, etc. I haven't suddenly changed and I'm not trying to rob them blind.

After maybe an hour or so, we seemed a little like partners again, but even then, they don't want to come off these points at all:

- They want to completely remove the 33% amount related to the taxes.
- They want the ROI to be calculated at 18 months.
- They want the 50/50 payout.

In short, they don't want to negotiate on these points at all.

By the end of the meeting they were at least smiling a little, but we didn't solve anything. I told them I'd try to think of something to do, but at this point all we can do is agree to disagree. I told them they had to be willing to compromise somewhere, or this just wasn't going to work, I can't agree with their offer.

As I think about everything tonight as I write this entry, I'm again reminded of Joe's advice: stall. I talked to the partners specifically about whether anyone was talking about quitting, and they said no, so hopefully I'm still safe with that tactic.

Based on our meeting, I also didn't get any ideas about what their lawyer might have told them, other than to stick to their guns with a lowball offer. There was nothing in our conversation to indicate that they've spoken to a lawyer.

We've sent a few emails of no consequence back and forth, so this evening I sent them another one. I wrote:

"Guys, I don't want to piss you off again, but I can't think of how to make this work for both sides. While reading this next option, please remember that I'm still the guy that has worked with you for the last five years, and the same guy that had breakfast with you last Thursday. I'm trying to make this work, and this is the best option I can think of.

Since we can't agree on a compromise, let's explore your offer again, and let's do it even better, let's take it all the way down to book value.

Since we know I want to leave at the end of April, what if we agree to keep everything as the status quo for right now, and then I will sell my shares to you at book value ('fire sale value') on February 28th of next year? At that time, I think that offer is a reasonable value to me, and it also serves the purpose of drastically reducing what you'd have to pay.

I promise to stay until at least April 30th, two months after the sale, and six months from today. We can also make an announcement to all the employees much earlier than this, let's say the first of the year.

Here's where I'm coming from: As I understand it, a big problem with the group of partners is trying to raise the kind of money that we're talking about, and as you know from all of our earlier buy/sell spreadsheets, this results in a much lower out of pocket number for all of you.

I think this is much more of a win/win situation. I get close to what I want, and for everyone who wants to buy my shares, you can get them at the lowest possible price.

I can talk to my lawyers, but we may even be able to sign a contract now stating these terms. That way you'll know I won't back out, I'll know you won't back out, and we can tell all the employees on January 1st that you are the new owners of the business.

I hope you'll consider this. At this point I can't accept your current offer, and I can't think of anything else to do, and I really want to sell my interest to you."

At this point I have no idea whether they'll go for this offer, but I really can't think of anything else to do. This isn't a stalling tactic, it's all I've got.

Well, for the third time since this started, I've really upset these guys, and this time I can't even understand why. What the heck was unreasonable about that offer? At this point they're not even saying anything rational. I thought they might counter with "January 31st" or "January 1st" as the transaction date, but they're not even saying anything like that.

At this point I'm getting pissed off about all of this myself. They don't want to negotiate at all, and it's like they've determined that their ace in the hole is for all of them to get irrationally upset about any offer, and presumably make me fear losing them. Screw them. At this point I don't really care if they all do quit. Admittedly I'd prefer if they waited a couple of months, but I don't know what else they want from me.

Unable to get them to come around to my way of thinking at all, I just told them it looks like we're at an impasse right now. I told them, "Maybe I'm not thinking about this right, but I think I am." I then told them that if we're really stuck here, and they're not willing to consider my offer, then I need to talk to some potential outside buyers. If those outside buyers tell me I'm way off base, then fine, maybe I should reduce my offer, but I told them if I were in their shoes, I would have taken this offer, no questions asked, and I really didn't understand their position. I feel like I'm doing everything I can to save them money, trying to help them buy a multimillion dollar business, and they just keep getting upset. I can't work with that.

After some terse and tense emails, we've finally agreed to a cooling off period.

From my perspective, the hardest parts about dealing with these guys is that they give me no feedback, and don't seem to understand the word "compromise." On the feedback issue, I still have no idea why they're upset with my last offer. I sent them another email offering the January 31st date, and got nothing back from them, other than it was unacceptable. I don't know why it's unacceptable, it just is. And no, I'm not going to offer than January 1st date.

They also prefer to communicate by email, and for me that takes a little while longer than just sitting somewhere with them and working through the numbers. At this point that's fine by me, as I'm still banking about $1K per day, but it seems like at some point we really should try to get a deal done.

Another major reason for the cooling off period is that we all agree that our work is suffering, and we need to shore it up before our customers notice. What's more likely is that they've already noticed, but just haven't said anything yet. We all agree that our business has a good reputation, and if these guys want to have something worth buying -- and not ruin their own reputations -- we better get some work done.

I really don't know where to go with this right now. At the moment we don't have a "next meeting" set up.

Not to be too much of an egomaniac here, but looking at the calendar, if I were these guys I'd be a lot more nervous now than I was at the beginning of September or October. As we've gone through these discussions, and I've thought more about what I want to do after I leave, I've made it clear that my last day will be April 30th, so there's now less than six months left before I leave.

Another three days have passed without any discussion or emails, and George and David wrote again today to see what I was thinking.

I wrote back and told them the truth, I can't think of anything else to offer them, and I think I need to talk to some potential outside buyers. I told them I'd made a list of five outside buyers, and I was going to find a way to approach. I told them I didn't have to sell all my shares to an outside buyer, but from what I've heard from our business broker and my lawyers, an outside buyer would almost certainly want controlling interest in the company. (And oh by the way guys, I was trying to sell that controlling interest to you.)

I asked again about the "book value" sale on January 31st, but again all that did was make them angry.

As I write this, I don't feel like I'm getting my emotion across here properly. It's not so much that I'm upset that they won't take my book value offer, it's more like I'm *flabbergasted* that they won't take it. I wrote them and asked them to please discuss that with their attorney, as it seems like an extraordinarily reasonable offer. I reiterated to them that we could sign papers as soon as possible to agree to these terms, and let the employees and our customers know that they have bought the business from me.

After today's emails, we again don't have a "next meeting" set up. Joe will be happy to know that the stalling part of the plan is working out really well.

The only thing to add here is that in their last email they asked me not to talk to any potential outside buyers yet. I told them I really can't wait very long, come hell or high water I'm leaving by April 30th, and outside buyers are going to need all the time they can get with me before I go.

Saturday, November 12, 2005

This past week was dominated by customer issues and opportunities with new prospects, so nothing has happened on the business selling front. I still haven't talked to Jack since our blowup (made easier by the fact that he's always at the office and I never am), so in the few new sales the company is making, George is getting all the practice he can working those situations with prospects. I expect him to ask for a raise if we can't get this business sale taken care of soon.

I met with George, David, and the other partners this morning, but the meeting was more somber than anything. Nobody seemed on the verge of quitting, but they did talk about sharpening their resumes. They didn't make it a threat as much as they made it a backup plan, meaning they weren't sending their resumes out, but they would be ready to jump ship if need be.

I wasn't too upset about that. Really, I'm amazed nobody has quit yet.

What I am still upset about is their absolute unwillingness to compromise. They still want the 33% discount, 18-month ROI, and the 50/50 payout. During the meeting I thought about reiterating the 16.5% compromise, and reducing the ROI to 21 months, and saying I wanted all the money up front, but frankly, with nobody threatening to quit, I'm not offering anything.

Again, my situation may be different from other business sales, but to be clear, my goal is to maximize the money I can get by April 30th, and I don't care how that happens.

The thing I'm really surprised about is that they don't seem to get this. Maybe they don't think I'll really leave ... I don't know. Regardless of what they think, I'm thinking, "Okay, you don't want me to talk to anyone outside the company, but you also don't want to negotiate, the days are ticking off the calendar, and I'm making $1K per day while we don't do anything ... um, okay. I can do this as long as you can."

We left the meeting without any agreement, other than assurances that nobody was quitting. However, George and Cooper all said time was of the essence, and we really needed to do something soon. I agreed with that assertion, and countered by saying that was why I needed to start talking to potential buyers outside the company.

I woke up in a very foul mood today. I think something one of the partners said at the meeting yesterday has upset me, but I don't remember any specific comment. I think it was more the general feeling that they expected me to do something, which was to compromise, without them compromising.

I woke up this morning, and thought, BS, I'll show them what compromise is. I packed a few things in my car, and drove out of town to stay at a hotel for a few days. I sent the Class A partners and our receptionist an email and said a personal matter had come up, and I had to go out of town for a few days.

It was mostly true, I had a personal matter: I was pissed. Thinking more like a "short timer" than a business owner, I also figured I had a lot of personal time I hadn't used over all these years, and I might as well start taking it.

Figuring I couldn't hold out forever, I came back into town late last night, and went to work this morning.

Another rule in negotiating is that, "The first person that talks loses," and while I'm very well aware of that rule, the partners didn't offer any sort of compromise in my absence, and despite what I've told them, me going to anyone outside the company is a bluff more than anything else.

Therefore, I just wrote them with some compromise terms, and said, "I'll agree to a 28% discount and 21-month ROI terms, but, all the money must be in cash, paid at the time of closing." I had put a salary request in my earlier spreadsheet $8,333/month after the sale ($100K/year), but I also increased that to $12K/month. I reiterated that I wanted all the miscellaneous items I wrote about before, plus a few more. I also told them that time was running out, and in addition to making this offer to them, I had no choice but to also start talking to people outside the company, and had already placed several calls.

In truth, if I wasn't consciously thinking about the lawyer's "stall" plan before, I'm totally on board now. Based on their past reactions, I don't expect them to agree to these terms, but I hope they'll see that I'm trying to do something, so they won't send their resumes out just yet.

I have to say, I'm also in a much better mood about this after getting away for a few days ... but I'm not in that good of a mood. If they counteroffer with their same BS lowball offer without any compromise, fine, they can lowball, and I can stall.

If it's not obvious from my writing, it's important to note that this has gotten very personal over the last few weeks. I feel like I started this process with good intentions, but with our expectations being so far apart, and having all these difficulties negotiating, I'm not sure I consider these guys to be "friends" any more, if some of us were even friends before. I still get along with David fairly well, and I try to remember that I liked him before, but I'm having a really hard time of thinking of the other guys as friends. I'm going to have a hard time rooting for them to succeed if I end up selling the company to them.

Blech ... another Saturday meeting with George and David. Admittedly I've been in an unhappy mood with these guys lately, and with all these recent weekend meetings the sarcastic part of me is thinking, "Where was all this interest in the company the last few years?"

I know that's not fair though. Just because they weren't always working at the office or a client site, that doesn't mean they weren't working, and I know how many hours they billed per week. If I'm angry at anything besides this process, it's just that I thought they never showed any interest in the *business* before; they were just interested in billing customers and therefore making more money for themselves. But again, I can't be too angry about that either, because that's a culture I helped create ... which I've come to regret.

Their offer

Today's coffee shop meeting wasn't hostile, but more of a counteroffer from them:

- A 30% discount (instead of my 28% offer) to account for how the taxes would affect their net income distributions.
- A 21-month ROI plan (unchanged from my offer).
- They reduced my salary after the sale back to $10K/month.
- They agreed that all money would be paid at closing time.
- All the smaller items I asked for.
- We also added a term that I would definitely agree to stay with the company until April 30th. Actually, what we discussed was that I wouldn't have to see Jack, and if he did anything to make my life miserable, I would leave whenever I wanted to.
- They wanted an agreement that my (former) wife would also stay at least a few months after the sale so they could find someone to replace her, but I told them that was her decision.

- In a bit of a surprise, they asked for a longer noncompete agreement from me, but I said no, I wouldn't do that at the price we're talking about right now.

They said they didn't have agreement from these terms from all of the other partners, but that they would share this with them. I noticed that they seemed much happier than I've seen them in a while, and frankly I'm very surprised they came to any compromise at all.

I told them I'd think about it, but I wasn't happy with the change from 28% to 30% along with the salary reduction, and I even stated the tax point was really pissing me off. I'd come down from 33% to just 5%, and I really thought it should be 16.5%. Since they seemed happy, I figured I might as well push back again.

Given my angst with them, I didn't bother to tell them about the personal goodwill clause just yet. That's still going to be my Columbo "Just one more thing" part when all the other terms have been agreed to.

In another note, I'm reminded that my former wife (and Jack's wife) don't have employment agreements with the company. My wife was Employee #2, and Jack's wife came on fairly early as well. Way back then we didn't see the need for agreements with them. I'm not going to mention it to these guys, but it was an amusing thought today.

I'll assume that David and George talked to the other partners over the weekend, I don't know for sure. Really, I'd be surprised if they didn't all know about that offer before, but if they did, I can't imagine a good reason for them to be taking their time. Maybe they're having some problems with their coalition, I don't know. They just seemed so happy, I assumed they'd come back right away.

Since they haven't come back with anything yet, I haven't bothered to get back with them about the 28% or 30% issue. All I know is that I'm heading home for Thanksgiving tomorrow morning, and nothing is going to happen this week.

It's a week later now, and all is still quiet, and I have to say, it's been a very welcome relief. Of course Thanksgiving was in there, and that was a break for everyone, but beyond that, David and George haven't come back with anything.

The suspicious part of me is wondering if they're all about to jump ship to start their own company, but I really don't think they'll do anything like that. While they're all very good at what they do technically, they wouldn't have all the parts they'd need to run a company, and I hope they've learned that through our discussions. They might get Jack to be their salesperson -- and maybe he's weaseled his way into this process -- but there's still so much more that they'd be missing, and so much they'd have to do by starting over again from scratch, I just can't see that happening.

In the actual process of working on client projects, I've been working with David most days, but we don't have any quiet time to discuss things, and I also don't want to put him on the spot. David is the one person I still think of as a friend, and his friendship is more important to me than selling the business to him. If I could find a way to do it, I'd sell him some shares at a discounted rate compared to the other business partners, but as I think about how to make that happen, that would only cause problems with the other partners.

At the moment I'm going to put the delay down to infighting in their coalition, or maybe some of them are trying to figure out how to come up with the money. Either way, I'm going to leave it at that. Thinking about this makes me wonder if they'll completely blow their tops when they hear about the goodwill clause. I'm tempted to say something to them about it now, but without any more information on what's going on, I'm still going to keep that to myself.

I'm also tempted to tell them that I have meetings coming up with buyers outside the company, but I don't think that's the right strategy.

With today being the last day of November, there's just one more month left in the year, and five full months before I leave.

While I wait to see if the partner coalition will eventually let me know whether they're going to make me an offer, I thought I'd share what I know about the "Goodwill Clause" my tax attorney told me about.

The first thing to say is that this isn't a clause that will work for just anyone. For instance, it wouldn't work for Jack. My tax attorney told me I'd be eligible for it for several reasons, including (a) I founded the company, (b) I give almost all of our public seminars and it's always my name in the media, and (c) when clients -- at least our large clients -- think about our company, they think about me. I've even heard stories that when people can't remember the name of our company they always refer to it as "Al's company."

Given these statements, the tax attorney said I would be eligible to qualify for this goodwill clause when selling my ownership interest. I've forgotten most of what he had to say about this clause, so I just dug through the notes I made during my meeting with him. Here are the bullet points from those notes:

- General rule: "Ordinary income is bad." Don't want to get $ as a consultant following my sale of the company because that is ordinary income. (My main lawyer suggested getting paid as a consultant after the sale, but the tax attorney said no, you're eligible for this goodwill option.)
- The phrase he used is something like "we want to characterize the purchase price as goodwill."
- The very important point: Payments characterized as goodwill are taxed at 15%. (By contrast, ordinary income would be taxed at the federal level of at least 33% for my income bracket.)
- I want as much of the sale price as possible to be characterized as goodwill. Not all of it will be eligible for goodwill because of my *basis* in the company.
- Regarding getting paid, he strongly recommends that I get all the money up front, but if I really have to, I can receive

installment payments, and these can still go against goodwill.

- Whoever buys my interest won't like this, because goodwill is depreciated over 10-15 years.

- Other money can, and should, go against my basis. For instance, if my basis in the company is $60K, I want $60K or more to go against that. In this case, the basis reduces what is effectively a capital gain.

I'm hoping I can get away with dropping this on the partners because, as you can see, it is a little complicated, and I won't even claim to understand it all at this time. So, I won't be lying whenever I tell them I don't completely understand it.

LLC capital accounts

On a related note, I haven't written much here about capital accounts. As I have written, our business is organized as an LLC, and each of the partners has something referred to as a "capital account."

A capital account tracks how much money is distributed to partners in an LLC. If you have your own LLC, you probably understand this already, and if not, you can easily find information about it on the internet, so I won't repeat all that here. My reason for bringing this up is to mention that even as we've been going through this negotiation process, we've still been taking out distributions every quarter as we normally would.

I can see how this could be a very real problem for other businesses to deal with when you have two business partners not talking to each other like Jack and I, so if you're looking at selling your own business, for the most part I suggest trying to keep distributions as normal as you can. Of course how that works will vary by circumstance, including what percent of the company you own and control.

As a final note about capital accounts, I've made it clear to these partners that my capital account is off limits. If I haven't mentioned it here yet, another term of the deal I added is that when I sell my interest, I expect the company to cut me a check for the amount in my capital account, or at least the amount the accountant says I am officially due. For instance, I may have a $100K balance in my capital account right now, but anyone who buys my interest doesn't get a dime of that, unless of course they want to pay me $100K for it. That money has essentially already been taxed, it's based on my current ownership, and in my opinion, they have absolutely no right to that money.

I don't remember when I did this, but at some point I added this to the documents we've been passing back and forth. I didn't make a big deal of it, I just wrote that this is the way it is, you can check with your attorney, but this is the right way to deal with this, and it's not negotiable. (When they agreed to this, I quit worrying that they would try to come back to me on this if I ended up stalling a lot.)

It's amazing what you learn in the process of selling a business.

My ex-wife still works as the bookkeeper, receptionist, and all-around manager back at the office, but we haven't talked about this sales process or the partners in a long time, at least not until a funny incident today.

She called me while I was at a client site and asked, "What are you doing to these guys?" I asked what she meant, and she told me someone from a neighboring business just came into our office, and frantically told her that two guys had just left our office, rear-ended another car, then drove off laughing. He wanted to know if he should call the police.

Once she got the details from him, including which car had been hit, she realized Jack and David had just left the office, and Jack rear-ended his wife's car in the parking lot. Apparently because he hit his wife's car, they didn't bother to stop and come back into the office, and just went to wherever they were going.

After we shared a laugh about this story, she asked a little more seriously how things were going, and told me that Jack and David were constantly running out for short, unannounced meetings. I told her I'd tell her all about it in time, but all the meetings were probably related to the sale, and my leaving.

Other than that last funny story, I deleted all the other diary entries between December 3rd and now because they were just a bunch of back and forth between the partners and myself, at first covering minor points about their last spreadsheet, and then of course the goodwill clause.

They complained a lot that I had already negotiated a sales price with them, and then dropped the goodwill clause on them, but I lied, and told them I had just learned about it from my tax attorney when discussing the 33% tax issue. They didn't know what it meant at first, so I told them to talk to their attorney about it, because my attorney couldn't talk to them, and I probably couldn't get the details right myself.

Once they more or less agreed to the goodwill clause, we next had to get it past our company accountant, who also happens to be my personal accountant. It took a couple of days for him to hook up with my tax attorney, and then agreed to it.

Of course at this point I had to tell the accountant what was going on, that I was planning to sell my interest to this group of partners, and that's where this clause came in. Until then I had kept him out of the loop, and apologized to him for that. I also told him that he was free to discuss the ramifications of this clause with these partners, since they would have to live with it after I was gone.

During this process I managed to leave town twice more, once for another excursion just to stall, and now this current break to visit with my family for the holidays. It also helped my cause that none of us were able to get quick responses from our attorneys. I thought my attorney might be moving slow to help my cause, but when their attorney moved slow too, I assumed they were just busy.

Formal Letter of Intent

After giving me a lot of grief, the partner coalition eventually agreed to the goodwill clause, in addition to "compromising" on the tax issue at 29%. (That still pisses me off, which is why I added more 'stall' days in here lately.) They finally got their Letter of Intent to buy shares drafted, and sent it to me by email yesterday.

I haven't mentioned how upset they have been with all these delays, but in short, feeling like I can't delay the process any more, and not really wanting to, I told them that for both sentimental and accounting reasons I would accept their offer formally as of December 31st, with the major stipulation that we had to finalize all the paperwork within two weeks of that time. I again emphasized that if this wasn't going to work out for some reason, I had very little time to get a deal done with outside people who were interested in buying the company.

I'm guessing that part of their recent anger is that they figured out what's been going on with the stalling tactic. They wanted to backdate everything back to December 10th, when we had agreed on many points, but I told them there was no way I was going to do that. I told them I really didn't agree with anything by that time, and that many of these delays were as much their fault as they were mine.

They also got upset again when I insisted the paperwork had to be completed by January 14th, but I reiterated that this needed to get done, or I needed to talk to people outside the company ASAP. I also suggested that this was in their best interest, because they really needed to start letting key customers know that I was leaving very soon. In reality, my only concern was that I didn't want to feel like I'd sold the company, and then have to wait forever to get the legal paperwork done.

I called my attorney to let him know that we had finally come to terms on an agreement, and also called our company attorney to let her know as well. They both assured me that we could get this done in the next two weeks, so I'm happy to say I'm sitting here in my hometown, typing this diary entry, and I'll be out of my business in four months, with a total compensation package I can finally agree to.

It took a little longer than desired, but we finally closed on the sale late this afternoon. After ten years as a successful small business owner ... I am no longer a small business owner. But, I am a guy who successfully sold his small business, and all the lawyers told me that's something that rarely happens.

I don't know if it's sunk in yet, but I'm sure it will sink in as soon as I don't get a quarterly distribution check. In the meantime, these nice, big six-figure closing checks will have to do.

There isn't much to say about the closing ... if you've been through the process of buying or selling a home, the process is painfully familiar. I basically agreed to sell my business to my business partners nearly three weeks ago, and we had to wait to have the lawyers catch up to us, and then sign all their legal documents today. In a couple of the documents they copied and pasted the terms of our agreement, and as far as I could tell, everything else was boilerplate stuff. I had my personal lawyer (Joe) review everything the company lawyer wrote up, and after some discussions between themselves, Joe told me everything was written to his satisfaction.

Since everyone was paying me in full at closing time our papers were probably easier than most business deals, so it really was just a matter of signing a bunch of legal documents. Once everything was signed and countersigned, each of the partners handed me personal checks that corresponded to the amount of shares they were buying, and it was over.

I can see where this would be much more complicated if there were going to be payments over time, or if I had agreed to stay for a longer period of time (twelve, eighteen months, or more), but since we didn't have those things it all felt very simple, if not lengthy.

I forgot to mention it here, but I wouldn't put in writing that I agreed to stay through April 30th. I told the partners I thought that might give Jack some sort of leverage, and I wouldn't go for it. I told them they had my word that as I long as I didn't have to work with Jack, and he didn't do anything to make life difficult for me (or my former wife), that I would stay until then.

I also need to mention that I was now going to be paid as a regular employee, and that I didn't have any sort of guaranteed contract. I would be paid a $10K/month salary as long as I was employed, but I wasn't guaranteed employment through April 30th. I couldn't imagine them letting me go, but who knows, we have been at odds for months now.

Finally, I refused to sign any other noncompete agreements. I had signed the Operating Agreement years ago, and it stated that I couldn't compete with the company for twelve months after the sale if I left, and despite the objections of the partner coalition, their lawyer, and Jack, I refused to sign anything else implying a noncompete agreement. I told them I gave them a big discount compared to an outside entity, and as a result I wouldn't sign a longer agreement.

At the end of the meeting I shook hands with all the lawyers and my former business partners, who were now my new bosses. The partners went out to celebrate, and I went out, bought a bottle of champagne and two nice cigars, and celebrated quietly by myself in a small park near my apartment, joined for a little while by a neighbor/friend who asked what I was doing.

After smoking just one of the cigars, I went inside and began packing like crazy. "It's finally over," I thought, and I'm ready to move on. I think the painful part will now be waiting here until April 30th, if I last that long.

But, first things first. I promised the partners I'd be there to tell all the employees what just happened, and I'd also be there to meet with some of our key customers to personally let them know I had sold my business to the partners, and that I'd be leaving town in a few months, and I will honor those agreements.

In a funny thing related to the closing process, a check I received from one of the partners bounced. I wrote him and told him about it, and said that was fine, I'd just go ahead and keep my ownership interest after all. He wrote me a new check the same day.

SATURDAY, JANUARY 28, 2006

We told the employees last Thursday about the sale, and at least for me, it didn't seem like a huge deal. We have fourteen full-time employees and four contractors right now, and because (a) there isn't a big change in regime, (b) I'm rarely at the office anyway, (c) several of these people are now partners in the business, I just don't think it affects these guys that much.

I guess I should back up and say that because I work with employees in the field much more, they seemed to have a much stronger reaction, but in the end it was all a bunch of well-wishes and "let's keep in touch" discussions.

This week we also had several meetings with key customers, and in their own way, they were more emotional for me than meeting with the employees. I've worked at all of their offices, and these clients and all of their employees have almost always been amazingly nice to me. I feel like I've been their guest, worked hard to win and keep their business, and it was now time to leave. In addition to that, many of these customers have been with me since the beginning, and that's been a long time. I feel this emotional tie to them, where I think that these people have helped make me and my company be successful.

Not to make this sound too much like the old television series *Cheers*, but last night I went to my favorite local bar, and shared the news with the people there who didn't already know what was going on. I bought margaritas and beer for everyone I knew, and for a few other well-wishers who happened to be in the right place at the right time.

The most interesting moment came when a friend asked if I felt like I had groomed a "successor," someone who I really felt comfortable selling my business to. I thought for a few moments, and shared the honest truth: I think they'll be fine without me, but no, I don't feel like I'm leaving the business to a "successor," to someone who's going to run the business the way I'd like to see it run.

That conversation made me think back through all the years, and I remember hoping at several points that I'd find a kindred spirit, someone who really shared my vision about how to run a business, something like a Ben & Jerry relationship ... but that person never materialized. I did sell my business to a group of people who had been my business partners, so I can be a little happy about that, but I didn't sell it to "The One"; this isn't *The Matrix*, and there was no Neo.

One problem has come up in the last few weeks that seems to be the nail in the coffin for my relationship with some of the partners, George in particular.

During the final detailed discussions back in December, we sent some spreadsheets back and forth related to handling certain accounting charges properly. To keep the story short, what happened from my perspective was that we passed these spreadsheets back and forth, and agreed that the five line items in the spreadsheet would be handled a particular way. We knew the numbers weren't exact, but we were all comfortable with them as estimates, and agreed to this spreadsheet.

The company accountant recently finished closing the books for the year, and I got an email from George with a new spreadsheet attached, showing two additional line items, and a message I read as, "Oh, by the way, you got the short end of the straw here by $5,000."

Technically, from an accounting perspective these two additional charges were correct, but I had perceived *our* spreadsheets as a gentleman's agreement, a handshake deal. As a result, I didn't handle George's email or this situation very well, and after a few emails where I tried to say that I thought we had a handshake deal on the *five* line items in our spreadsheet, I blew my top, went over the line and immediately questioned George's integrity (which was in part triggered by the language in his email to me). Suffice it to say, we didn't even attempt to negotiate the difference, and I'm not speaking with George these days either.

The thing that upset me about this is that a long time ago, when George first became a partner, there was a misunderstanding between us related to the tax consequences of him being a partner, specifically how health insurance would be accounted for. I don't remember all the details, but because he was now a partner, the amount he paid for health insurance was treated differently from a tax perspective, and it ended up costing him more money than either of us expected for him to be a partner.

When I learned about this problem -- a tax consequence I knew nothing about then, and barely know the details of today -- I didn't tell him, "That's how accounting works, sorry for your luck," I just asked him how much money this misunderstanding cost him, wrote him a check for that amount, and said I was sorry, I didn't know about that detail.

When he refused to compromise on the $5,000 that worked to his advantage, I sent him an email about this old situation, and he wrote back something to the effect, "Sorry, I don't remember that situation."

Asshole.

The way this worked out financially is that we kept a small amount of money related to the sale in escrow, assuming those five spreadsheet line items would work out one way or another, and I would owe the partners *a little* money, or they would owe me some. So I didn't have to write them a check for $5,000, but I got less money out of our escrow funds than I expected.

SUNDAY, APRIL 30, 2006

Somewhere along the way I managed to look at the calendar for the wrong year: This year the 28th was the last Friday in April, and was therefore my last day with the company.

My clients kept me very busy these last few months, but during this last week they all took time to say goodbye to me one way or another, including several free lunches. Today my current client gave me another going away party at lunch, and then I packed the belongings I had at their office in the afternoon.

Afterwards my partners had a going-away party for me at a local bar/restaurant, where I said goodbye to everyone I had once hired. I didn't speak to Jack or George during the party, but as I left the party I did take a moment to thank Jack for his year's of hard work. As I leave I may not be happy with the man, but he did a lot for the company in the early years.

That party with my former employees and coworkers was followed by another party at the bar by my apartment (okay, there's been a party there every night this week), then additional parties with friends on Saturday and again today.

To cap off a very emotional week, I managed to launch a web browser yesterday morning, and while I intended to look at something else, I accidentally went to my former company's webmail page. I sat there for a few moments, looking at the login screen, and then it really hit me -- I'm not welcome to log in there any more. I don't work there any more, and if everyone is doing their job in a timely manner, my username and password shouldn't work.

I took a screenshot of the login page, closed that tab on my browser, and deleted all the browser bookmarks I had set for my company and our client's websites. If I was looking for a defining moment that said it was all over, this was certainly it.

Moving on

I think the legendary baseball player Satchel Paige once said, "Don't look back, something might be gaining on you," and I've lived by that philosophy for many years, long before this process. So after that brief emotional moment yesterday morning, everything else has been a celebration, with a focus on moving forward.

I'm currently packing my car with everything I want to keep, selling everything else through Craigslist, and after taking care of a few more personal details tomorrow, I'll be getting on the road first thing Tuesday morning.

My current plan is to spend the rest of the week with family and friends in Illinois, then hop in the car the following Monday. I'll drive across the country at whatever pace I want, and eventually cross the border into Canada and take the ALCAN to Alaska. Whatever happens after that ... well, it happens. For the first time in a very long time, there are no future plans.

APPENDIX A: FINANCIAL ASSUMPTIONS

In fictionalizing the financial portion of my company, two key values were necessary, Revenue Per Employee, and Net Income. I'll look at Net Income first, and then Revenue Per Employee.

Net Income Assumptions

Many, many years ago I learned about a company named Robert Morris Associates, a business that provides financial data about existing businesses. Since the last time I looked at their information that business has become a company named Risk Management Associates (still using the acronym "RMA"), but they still publish the same financial information about businesses, organized by NAIC code.

I went to the local library, found the RMA Annual Statement Studies, and found *Net Profit* ratios of 16.3% and 15.3% for Custom Computer Programming and Computer Systems Design Services NAIC codes, respectively, for healthy businesses. Trying to keep the numbers in this book simple, I chose a fictional Net Income value of 15% for this story.

Revenue Per Employee Assumptions

The second assumption I needed to use to fictionalize the financial values for this story is a ratio of *Revenue Per Employee*. By using (a) this value and (b) stating that we had fifteen or twenty employees, I could easily derive a Yearly Revenue value for my company.

I documented my Revenue Per Employee findings on the devdaily.com website, so I won't bother to repeat them all here, other than to say that I found these numbers from several well-known computer service firms:

- CACI - $169K/employee
- Accenture - $133K to $155K/employee (depending on the source)
- EDS - $131K/employee
- Perot Systems - $108K/employee

While these numbers are a little scattered (Perot Systems seems like an outlier, which may be why they were bought by Dell), I decided to use the approximate average of these Revenue Per Employee values for my story. The actual average of those values is $139.2K, which I rounded up to $140K.

(As an interesting side story, if you'll look at the Revenue Per Employee statistics on the devdaily site, you'll see that this ratio is fairly consistent within an industry, but if you look at other industries, you'll see that Apple and Google make roughly $1.2M/employee, while oil companies have an even higher ratio than those businesses.)

In summary, all of the financial numbers presented in this book come back to these two financial assumptions:

- 15% Net Income
- $140K Revenue Per Employee

When I first wrote this story, I ended it with the Financial Assumptions chapter, but after receiving many comments on my website asking, "What happened after the sale? How do you feel now?", I decided to add several new sections about the years that followed the sale.

Three days after my last day of employment with the company I founded, I finished cleaning out my apartment, my car was packed, and I began the drive to Alaska, stopping in Illinois first to visit with my family.

After visiting with my family for a few days -- and nearly breaking my right hand by accidentally using a softball bat in a 70 mph baseball batting cage -- I hopped in my car and slowly drove to Alaska, working my way to Seattle, and then driving north through British Columbia and the Yukon Territory in western Canada on a road known as the ALCAN, or Alaska Highway. The timing of my trip couldn't have been any better. I saw more than one hundred bears along the roadsides, along with an amazing amount of wildlife, and unbelievable scenery I had never seen before. Taking my time to enjoy the scenery, I finally arrived in Anchorage, Alaska fifteen days after leaving Illinois.

I fooled around in Anchorage for a few days before deciding to really stay in Alaska for a while, so I started looking around for a place to rent. It just so happens that tens of thousands of people move to Alaska every summer, and nice places are hard to come by in May. With only a few good options, I decided to go for the full monty and continue to scare myself, so I rented a small cabin in Talkeetna, Alaska, population 800 people during the summer months, and about half that during the winter months. To give you some frame of reference, Talkeetna is two hours north of Anchorage (when the weather is nice), and the closest McDonalds is about seventy miles away.

Alaska is a wonderful place, but I won't bore you here with those details. If you're interested in learning about my adventures up there, check out my OneMansAlaska.com and AlaskaSquirrel.com websites.

After living in Alaska from late mid-May until late August, waking up and going to sleep whenever I wanted, growing out my hair and beard, surviving forest fires that were larger than major metropolitan areas like St. Louis, realizing that electricity and indoor plumbing weren't givens, and exploring every part of Alaska you could drive to, including the road the Ice Road Truckers take up to Prudhoe Bay (the Dalton Highway), one day I realized I was refreshed, and ready to get back to work doing ... well, something.

This revelation came to me after taking a sled dog ride in Seward, Alaska in August. Twelve "Alaska huskies" pulled eight people on a large dog sled that had wheels instead of skis. A training trail had been cut through the forest, and running the dogs like this not only makes for a great tour, it also helps keep the dogs in shape. After a few miles the driver (musher) pulled over by the side of a river to let the dogs rest. In the summer Alaska "heat" of about fifty degrees, the dogs were panting hard, with long tongues hanging from every mouth. As I looked at them, I couldn't see how they could possibly go on.

While they rested, all the tourists walked around the forest, went down by the river, and took photos. When we came back to the sled, much to my surprise, the dogs were ready to go once again, jumping up and down, ready to pull the sled as hard as they could.

That's when it hit me -- I felt exactly the same way. Several months ago I was exhausted, and I didn't feel like I could go on, but now I was refreshed, and ready to go back to work once again.

I checked in with all my friends and relatives to see what everyone was up to, to see if anyone wanted to explore any business ideas with some of my newfound wealth. I explored several ideas, but none of them blew me away, so I stayed in Talkeetna, trying to think of what I should do next.

By this time it was mid-September, and was my habit, every day I took a walk through town and then down to the river. However, things were changing, the morning temperatures were getting colder and colder, often beginning in the twenties, but most importantly, every day it seemed like another store had a sign up, "Closed for the winter."

Until then I didn't realize that most people left for the winter, and suddenly I felt scared in a different way: I'm pretty much a city boy, and being stranded in Talkeetna, Alaska for a winter with just a few hundred other people freaked me out. Really, it didn't scare me too bad, but combined with the small cabin, and the thousands of dollars I'd need to spend to survive the winter there, I decided to leave.

I paid the early cancelation fees with my landlord, traveled around Alaska for a little while longer, and finally left the state on the last day of September. Once again I saw dozens of bears while driving through Canada, saw many incredible sites that most people can only dream about, and to my great surprise, I ended up back in Kentucky several weeks later.

I ended up in Kentucky again for two main reasons. First, I kept trying to explore new business ideas with friends and relatives, but none of those panned out. I either wasn't sold on the ideas I heard, or people didn't want to leave their current situations to try to start a new business. The second big reason I ended up back in Kentucky had to do with the economy. I could tell the economy was going south, and lacking any new ideas, and thinking it was a good idea to keep making money, I went back there to work with my former customers.

One of the amusing things about my former company's Operating Agreement was that a partner could only compete with the firm "one year after the sale of the business." The funny thing here is that I although I left the business at the end of April, I sold it in January, so by January of the following year -- only two months away -- I'd be able to work again, right where I was before.

Lest you think this is evil, keep in mind that several unpleasant things happened with my old business partners during and after the sale, not all of which I've documented here. I didn't do this for revenge, I did it for the money, but yes, some part of me thought it was pretty amusing. Between using a standard, off the shelf Operating Agreement, and by staying at the company after the sale, my noncompete agreement was more lenient than a standard employee's noncompete agreement.

On a personal note -- whatever this says about me -- music became interesting again during this process. When my wife and I separated, I listened to Faith Hill songs for a while, and then after selling the business and driving to Alaska, I found that many of Christina Aguilera's songs were uplifting and often about freedom. In Alaska, I discovered the Dixie Chicks, and I can tell you where I heard each of their songs for the first time. For years I had little interest in new music, but during and after the sales process, I was suddenly open again.

Nothing major changed for me during this next year. I continued to provide consulting services, but I didn't hire any employees, and just worked by myself. This was a very low-stress approach to working, and I was still making a healthy salary. With the economy tanking rapidly, I decided to keep doing this until I came up with a better idea.

Although *my* life was uneventful, two things happened with my former company. First, when I left, we had a large "retainer" with one of our clients, and it was time for my former company to repay that retainer. This wasn't a retainer so much as it was a deposit, and while all the partners in the company knew about it, some of them apparently "forgot" about it during the sales process.

I had no idea they had forgotten about it, and in fact, it never came up during our discussions. I know they all knew about it, and as Jack liked to say, he was our "CFO," so he *really* knew about it. To make a long story short, they all really know about it now, and are upset that this large amount of money needs to be repaid to the client.

This leads into the second thing that happened with my former company: At least some part of it was resold to an outside entity, some people from Virginia. I don't know those people, and I don't know the details of the transaction, other than hearing that Jack had sold all of his interest in the company, and that he and his wife left the company a few months after the sale. I do know that he didn't leave the company before that retainer issue was discovered, but I don't know how they resolved that problem.

They tried to contact me by email, but I ignored their emails. Given the fact that I felt screwed by the partners when they went with "pure accounting" instead of "intent" during my last months with the company -- and I took a $5,000 hit -- I didn't feel any obligation to reply to them. My only reply would have been something like "As you know, accounting is accounting," but after checking with my lawyer, I didn't even bother to reply.

Despite the poor economy, I decided to take a chance this year, quit the consulting business once again, and dedicated myself to writing for one of my websites, devdaily.com. Several factors encouraged this decision, including the simple fact that the more I wrote, the more traffic kept hitting the website, and it kept making more money. Beyond that, I looked at this website as finally being one project that I could really immerse myself into, trying to make something of real quality.

An additional factor here is that if you fall in love with Alaska, it never gets out from under your skin, so with it still calling me, I once again sold most of my belongings, packed what was left, and drove across country, this time ending up in a little town where they hold the State Fair: Palmer, Alaska.

I did everything I could to grow the devdaily site, which was now getting millions (and millions) of page views per year, and also created OneMansAlaska.com and AlaskaSquirrel.com. At some point I started thinking about publishing these diary notes, and one day noticed that the domain name HowISoldMyBusiness.com was available, so I grabbed it.

Unfortunately I got sick during this year, and after losing almost forty pounds in six weeks, the doctors finally decided that the problems were related to my gallbladder. I had my gallbladder removed in Anchorage, but then had a postoperative infection, and didn't recover from the initial infection for nearly a month. I continued to have pain and digestive problems for many months, until things finally returned to something close to normal.

It wasn't all bad, though. Along with developing my websites, I bought a nice bicycle and road hundreds of miles around Alaska, in addition to again driving around the entire state.

As I write these words, it's a little more than five years after I sold my company, and in addition to publishing this book, I'm also in the process of starting a new nonprofit, 501(c)(3) charitable company. Unfortunately I haven't received approval from the IRS for that business yet, so I can't tell you what it is, but the important thing is that it feels like something that's much more important than anything I've ever done in my life. While all my previous efforts generally boiled down to making as much money as I possibly could every year, this new effort is important to me, and it feels like it could leave a legacy that I'll be proud of.

As you can tell from my notes, it's taken five years for me to find this idea, but except for the gallbladder problem, it's been a great five years. I'm trying not to bore you with all the details of my explorations, so I'll just say it this way: I recently crossed the last items off of my "bucket list," and for months I haven't been able to think of anything I wanted to add to a new bucket list. It's a weird feeling for me, but I'm fairly content.

Some friends I've kept in touch with over the last five years asked me to make sure that I mentioned that I'm not the same person I was five years ago, and according to them, I'm not like them. I wake up when I wake up, go to sleep when I go to sleep, I usually don't know what day of the week it is, or what day of the month it is, etc. A drive on the ALCAN is supposed to be a "once in a lifetime" experience, but I've traveled back and forth on it twice now, spending weeks exploring the Canadian wilderness as well as Alaska.

I also work wherever I want to, and the final edits for this book took place in many places, including Santa Fe and Los Alamos, New Mexico and Boulder, Colorado, where I now live. Sections of this book have been written in every vacation spot you can imagine. The running joke on Facebook is that every time I post a photo on Facebook, people have to ask where I am today.

I don't write all of this to brag, I write it to say that I don't live the normal American lifestyle any more. Admittedly for a little while after selling my company I *completely* checked out of the American way of life, but these days I've just checked into a different way of life.

My reason for sharing this is to tell you that if you make enough money by owning your own business, and perhaps on the sale of your business, you too can live this type of lifestyle, if that's something you want to do.

I hope my nonprofit business idea is approved by the IRS and then becomes a success, but even if it doesn't, these last five years have been the best years of my life since I was a teenager, and I don't know if that's something most adults can say.

I hesitated to write this chapter for a long time, because I don't feel like I can offer advice for every business, every business situation, or every person, certainly not without knowing more about you. Every situation is unique.

My situation is that I started a business in my basement, grew it to fifteen employees and five contractors, got tired of not being able to grow the business beyond that, had problems with my business partners, got divorced, found myself living in a city I didn't want to live in, but I was also making a lot of money every year.

I don't know what your situation is, but with that caveat, here's a summary of the lessons I learned during and after the sale of my business.

1) Have someone you can talk to

In my situation, I had a few people I could talk to, including family members and old friends. I was fortunate to have friends like this that I could talk to, and if anything, they helped keep me at the business longer.

If you're a business owner, you may know this next feeling, but with my business partners, David included, I never felt I could 100% trust them or their advice. Maybe it's just me, but I found it hard to have that 100% trust when they looked to me for their paycheck.

After I sold the business, a small part of me wished I had talked to a shrink or "life coach," but even then, I knew I was going something that wasn't making me happy. By late 2005, I had looked into the future, and it either meant continuing to do the work I was already doing in the field, or working a lot from the office, and those situations didn't appeal to me any more.

2) Think about this even more if you have a family

I don't have any children, and after the separation from my wife, I had no attachments in the area, so leaving the business was easy, it didn't affect anyone else.

The opposite of this situation is that you my have a spouse and children, and if so, I just encourage you to think about their lives, and what your income means to them. I don't want to encourage you to continue doing something you strongly dislike, but if it's something you *think* you like, and you're just burned out, I encourage you to take a sabbatical before making the decision to sell your company.

3) Find our whether you're just burned out

As I shared in my sled dog story, I knew for sure a few months after I moved to Alaska that I had been burned out, and by that time I felt fully recovered. In my situation, I knew this a little bit beforehand, but I probably didn't realize how bad the situation was.

It's possible that a wiser thing for me to have done would have been to say to everyone, "Guys, I'm burned out, I've been going at this really hard for ten years now, and I need a break." I could have then negotiated the terms of a sabbatical, and gone away for a while.

In retrospect I have thought about this a few times in the first few years. But these days I'm very happy with what I'm doing (and I'm extremely excited about my new nonprofit venture), and had I stayed, I would have had to work out the situation with Jack and his wife.

Speaking of Jack ...

4) Make sure you can get rid of partners

Regardless of how it happens, situations may come up where you think a partner can no longer fulfill his or her duties. In that case, you need to be able to do something about that situation, including having a way to get that person out of the company.

If you're just starting a business, and you're the majority owner or sole owner, I strongly encourage you to have clauses that allow you to buy out *all* partners at book value. In my case, I could only do this with Class B partners, and with the legal provisions related to Class A partners, I couldn't easily get rid of Jack. Trying to get rid of him would have torn apart the company.

Speaking of which ...

5) Don't keep spouses in the business too long

I can certainly understand the need to have spouses in the business, especially when you first get started. My wife fulfilled many roles, including bookkeeper, receptionist, and office manager, and those roles were incredibly helpful to us. Although she wanted to leave when we got to ten employees, Jack constantly talked her into staying.

Jack's wife represented a problem of a different kind. As I've mentioned here, in my opinion she became more valuable to the company than Jack, and this created a problem when I tried to buy out his interest. I tried to manage this the best I could, and even told him I'd sell her some interest once I bought his, but he wouldn't have any of it.

Beyond this, it also creates a real conflict of interest if there are problems between a spouse and other employees at a company. I always shared my feelings with my guys very directly, and if I thought they did poor work I let them know. But that's a much harder situation to deal with regarding your spouse, or someone else's, so again, good luck.

6) Don't settle for less than what you think the company is worth, you'll regret it

I pushed the guys I sold the business to as hard as I possibly could because (a) I had a price in my mind I thought the business was really worth, (b) I thought their initial price was way too low, and (c) I knew I'd regret it if I sold the business for less than that amount.

Looking back, I don't ever regret selling the business, the only thing I really miss about it is the big income I was making. Along with that, I know I would have regretted selling the business if it didn't feel like a win/win (or lose/lose) situation.

7) Selling is like playing poker, and you can overplay your hand

As a corollary to the previous point, selling your business can be like playing poker, but your business is at stake, and if you're not careful, the whole thing can blow up.

There's a phrase in poker about "overplaying your hand," and you have to be really careful about that. If you know the history of Apple, you know that before they brought Steve Jobs back in 1997, they almost went with another former Apple employee named Jean-Louis Gassé, but it's reported that Gassé thought he had the best operating system around at that time, and overplayed his hand by asking for way too much money, and Apple brought back Mr. Jobs.

8) If you're planning to retire, make sure you can live off the money you'll have after the sale. Don't let a financial analyst sweet-talk you into a dream of making 8% a year off your money.

I've worked with several financial advisors over the years, and in the end, I've never been really happy with any of them. If someone is telling you that you can make 5% or 10% on your money for the rest of your life, do yourself a favor and throw away their spreadsheets and create your own, using these assumptions:

- You won't make any interest on your money.
- Inflation will average at least four percent per year.

As you know from the difficult times we've had in the U.S. from 2007 through 2012, it can be really hard to earn interest on your money. I invested money through a professional money manager after the sale, and promptly lost a significant chunk of it. Fortunately I also made my own investments in stocks like Apple have done very well, but I've come away from experiences with money managers and financial planners with these thoughts:

- Don't believe that they can get you 6-8% per year for the rest of your life.
- Learn how to invest for yourself. It will be one of the most important things you can do to secure your financial future.

Based on those two thoughts, I currently let my money managers make my conservative investments for me (bonds and REITS, things that don't interest me very much), and I manage the majority of my money myself.

9) The act of selling is the first step in the act of quitting, and affects your decision making process

Mentally, the simple act of putting your business up for sale is a way of quitting. That may seem obvious, but I think it affects you in many small and subtle ways.

I always wondered if it affected Jack's attitude, that maybe he thought we would sell the business soon ... I don't know. (Just as likely, he wasn't happy with what his role at the company had become, and since we couldn't find enough good employees, he didn't have much to sell.)

In my own case, I found it affecting many decisions. I can clearly recall interviewing several employees and thinking, "We could sell this business next month, I hope I'm not messing with this person's future." It also affected other decisions, such as whether we should put a team together to buy office space, or continue leasing (which we did).

10) Find a business broker you like, who works in your industry

While Marty is a good guy and I enjoyed working with him, it's my opinion that his lack of connections in our industry limited us. His initial postcard encouraged me to take the steps to sell the business, but once I made the decision to sell, I should have talked to other brokers.

If you've worked with well-connected salespeople, you probably know this is true. A salesperson without contacts has to go through a lot of work just to find the right person to talk to, while a well-connected salesperson can pick up the phone and talk to the decision makers at businesses in just a few minutes.

11) Take the tombstone test

If you've never heard of the "tombstone test," it goes like this: Imagine that you're dead, and then imagine what you'd like written on your tombstone; what would you want written there?

In my case, by the mid-2000s I could have cared less that I was a successful small business owner, or that I was working in the software industry. While these things seemed important to me in the early 1990s, certainly by 2005 they were irrelevant.

It's not like I was doing anyone a huge favor as a business owner: If employees were great, I kept them, and if they sucked, I didn't. Great workers can always find another job, and the best thing I did was try to gather them together in one spot, and find interesting work for them. Doing that, along with solving problems for the customers I cared about, yes, those were important things, but they weren't important enough any more.

As I've mentioned before, these days writing this book is important to me, and once I've finished it, starting my nonprofit business will be the next very important thing to me. Ten years from now, who knows what the most important thing will be.

12) Find good attorneys

As I mentioned, I paid my tax attorney about $1,000 during this process, and he saved me tens of thousands of dollars. That was obviously a great investment.

Beyond that, my ability to work with my regular attorney (Joe) was also very important. I spent much more time working with Joe, and he was a great sounding board for everything related to the process, and it felt great to have an aggressive attorney looking out for my interests throughout the sales and closing process. He came up with the "stall" tactic that also netted me thousands of dollars, and he was a no-B.S. person who had been through this process before, knew what he was doing, and didn't waste my time.

Before starting the process of selling my business I avoided lawyers like the plague, but during the last six months of ownership, and during the sales process, I found that dealing with lawyers is just like anything else in business: Hire well, and you won't regret it.

More Information

For more information on anything related to this book, please visit the book's companion website, HowISoldMyBusiness.com. If you'd like to reach me, you can contact me using the website's contact form.

You can also find my work at other websites, including:

- alvinalexander.com (formerly devdaily.com)

- OneMansAlaska.com (stories from my life in Alaska)

- AlaskaSquirrel.com (a children's story about living in Alaska)

- My new business venture, Valley Programming (ValleyProgramming.com)

- My new nonprofit venture at ZenFoundation.org

You can also find me at twitter.com/alvinalexander.

15831021R00145

Printed in Great Britain
by Amazon